SPIRITUAL LEADERSHIP TODAY

Other Books by Mel Lawrenz

Putting the Pieces Back Together:
How Real Life and Real Faith Connect

Patterns: Ways to Develop a God-Filled Life

SPIRITUAL LEADERSHIP TODAY

HAVING DEEP INFLUENCE
IN EVERY WALK OF LIFE

MEL LAWRENZ

FOREWORD BY SKYE JETHANI

Previously published as *Spiritual Influence*

ZONDERVAN®

ZONDERVAN

Spiritual Leadership Today
Copyright © 2012, 2016 by Melvin E. Lawrenz III
Previously published as *Spiritual Influence*

This title is also available as a Zondervan ebook.

Requests for information should be addressed to:
Zondervan, 3900 Sparks Dr. SE, Grand Rapids, Michigan 49546

This edition: ISBN 978-0-310-52331-4 (softcover)

All Scripture quotations, unless otherwise indicated, are taken from The Holy Bible,
New International Version®, NIV®. Copyright © 1973, 1978, 1984, 2011 by Biblica, Inc.®
Used by permission of Zondervan. All rights reserved worldwide. www.Zondervan
.com. The "NIV" and "New International Version" are trademarks registered in the
United States Patent and Trademark Office by Biblica, Inc.®

Published in association with MacGregor Literary Agency.

Cover design: Rob Monacelli
Cover illustration: iStockphoto.com / yhloon
Interior design: Ben Fetterley and Matthew Van Zomeren

Printed in the United States of America

16 17 18 19 20 /DHV/ 20 19 18 17 16 15 14 13 12 11 10 9 8 7 6 5 4 3 2 1

This book is dedicated to Stuart Briscoe
and (in memoriam) John Stott.
Influencers extraordinaire.

CONTENTS

Part 3
GOING DEEP

Part 4
FACING CHALLENGES

FOREWORD

Not long ago a successful pastor of a large congregation was interviewed about his philosophy of leadership. "What is uniquely spiritual about your leadership?" he was asked.

"There's nothing distinctly spiritual," he responded. "I think a big problem in the church has been the dichotomy between spirituality and leadership. I grew up in a culture where everything was overly spiritualized," he added. This attitude, he said, caused many Christians to excuse ineffectiveness and waste by their leaders simply because they were nice, well-meaning, or people of prayer.

Instead he has adopted the belief that good leadership is rooted in the right principles which may be discovered in any sphere — business, government, or church. In his words, "A principle is a principle, and God created all the principles."

Once the idea that some leadership models are spiritual and other models unspiritual was abandoned, the gates were opened to adopt effective models from virtually anywhere. And that is exactly what has happened over the last thirty years. But has our desire for effective leadership principles been an overreaction to the abuses and ineptitude of earlier generations of Christian leaders? Have we been too eager to dismiss the spiritual dimensions of genuine Christian leadership? After all, while secular leadership principles are often deemed effective at growing corporations, generating revenue, or creating brand loyalty, can they be deployed as effectively toward the work of God's kingdom, which is not of this world? We are not called to simply sell Christ the way one sells Coca-Cola or Chryslers. Are we?

And what about the shortcomings of corporate culture? Studies indicate that workers within American corporations have a lower quality of life, higher divorce rate, and greater likelihood of developing clinical depression. And the ethical record of corporate America is probably not something the church would like to mimic. Reputable names like Enron, Anderson Consulting, AIG, Bear Stearns, Lehman Brothers, BP, and News Corp have been soiled, and in some cases buried, by ethical scandals driven by the bottom-line values, and indeed the leadership principles, of their managers.

The tarnished reputations of corporations, governments, and large organizations in general have made more people question the validity of secular leadership models. And in response to the pragmatism of the baby boomers within the church, a younger generation of Christian leaders is now emerging that seriously questions the wisdom of embracing and employing leadership values simply because they've proven effective in secular settings. They might agree that "a leadership principle is a leadership principle" if one's only criterion is effectiveness. But this risks deteriorating into a wholly unchristian utilitarianism where the ends justify the means.

Instead, when examining the ministry of Jesus, the apostles, or the patriarchs, one discovers that faithfulness often trumps mere effectiveness. And adhering to the countercultural, often counterintuitive values of God's kingdom will cause a leader to make decisions incomprehensible to those without the mind of Christ. And so many of the younger leaders with whom I engage are asking themselves — what is uniquely *Christian* leadership? And how does it differ from leadership in other realms? And if our struggle is not against flesh and blood, but "against the authorities, against the powers of this dark world and against the spiritual forces of evil in the heavenly realms" (Eph. 6:12), then how can our leadership not contain a uniquely spiritual component?

To answer these questions we need a wise teacher — one who understands the historical continuity of Christian leadership from

Jesus Christ onward, and yet recognizes the useful contribution more recent generations have made with their bent toward pragmatism. We have such a teacher in Mel Lawrenz.

Mel has been the senior pastor of a large church and has employed the tools necessary to lead an organization with hundreds of moving parts. In this capacity he has benefited from the practical wisdom of other leaders both inside and outside the church. But he has never lost sight of the uniquely spiritual dimension to our calling as servants of Jesus Christ. In this book he addresses the way character, prayer, communion with God, discernment, Scripture, and the Holy Spirit all impact our ability to influence those we lead. In other words, Mel Lawrenz sees the uniquely spiritual reality of Christian leadership without abandoning its practical application.

Mine is a generation of Christians eager to bridge the gap between our increasingly post-Christian culture and the present reality of God's kingdom. And we're not simply doing it through the institutional church. I have been encouraged by faithful women and men seeking Christ's calling in business, the arts, government, education, media, and the social sector. But we need help understanding how to lead effective, transformative change in these callings.

For that reason I am incredibly grateful for *Spiritual Leadership Today*. This book is not only helpful to anyone wanting to understand what is distinctive about Christian leadership, but by drawing from a wide range of historical sources, it also provides the reader a sense of context and continuity within the larger community of the church.

And those who thoughtfully engage this book will no doubt find themselves encouraged. Mel Lawrenz's perspective gives us hope that the leadership pendulum which has swung from overspiritualized to despiritualized in recent generations may have finally come to rest where it has always belonged—upon Jesus Christ.

—Skye Jethani, November 2011

ACKNOWLEDGMENTS

In the past few years during which I have been working on this book, many people have engaged with me in discussions about spiritual influence. I have learned so much and have been especially glad to hear from younger leaders about their concerns and aspirations. I am grateful for their honesty and their longing to see authentic forms of influence and leadership be the norm in the future.

My publishing partners have been incredibly thorough and dedicated. Thanks to Angela Scheff, Ryan Pazdur, Andrew Rogers, Brian Phipps, Chip MacGregor, and Joe Sherman. I am so grateful for your work and for making me work harder.

I'm grateful for the support of leaders at Elmbrook Church who have encouraged me to put time and energy into writing, traveling, and speaking in order to share our blessings.

As is always the case when I write a book, I benefited enormously from the wisdom of my wife, Ingrid, as we talked through the issues in this book before, during, and after the time when words were committed to paper. You have a most generous and good heart.

TO THE READER

Fifty years ago, J. Oswald Sanders, the director of a major mission organization in Asia, wrote *Spiritual Leadership*, a book that became a classic. I have met Christian leaders all over the world who consider the Sanders book a core definition of what they aspire to be and to do. Chuck Colson called it "the best book on Christian leadership I've read." The first time I was chosen to be a leader in the college campus ministry I was part of, the outgoing main leader gave me the Sanders book and said, "Read this. It is the baseline of everything you will do as a Christian leader."

Sanders' principles still apply, but there are new dynamics in the twenty-first century that offer us great new opportunities and previously unforeseen challenges.

I wish to offer some fresh thoughts in this book, *Spiritual Leadership Today*, not at all to contradict what Sanders said in his classic book but to engage with new realities in the twenty-first century. For example, people today are so longing for authenticity in their leaders that they will sniff out fakery from a hundred miles away. Also, today we use amazing new communication tools—podcasts and blogs and radio and TV, to name just a few—which allow us to contact much larger groups of people, but which also can be used to hide. And today people are looking for real-life wisdom that goes to the deep issues of life. They don't just want leaders to tell them what to do; they want leaders who will impart wisdom so that they themselves will be able to figure out what to do.

So why write a book called *Spiritual Leadership Today*?

The main reason I wanted to write this book is that I have a heart for all of you who take the daily risk to step into those most sensitive areas of other people's lives—their relationship with God, their spiritual lives, their struggles and aspirations, the challenges of being good influences in other people's lives. Whether you are a pastor or an educator or a manager or a healthcare worker or a parent, when you try to help people with their spiritual lives, you are stepping into the place where their greatest frustrations and greatest potentialities lie. You are steppping into the inner sanctuary of other people's lives.

This is a challenging call. It means we will be pushed and pulled by people's expectations, pressured by their criticisms, wounded by their opposition. We will have to deal with our own failures and know how to persevere through our setbacks and disappointments. But here is the irony: we are at our strongest in spiritual leadership when people see us dealing well with adversity. Part 4 of this book, "Facing Challenges," includes the chapters "Manage Expectations," "Persevere and Plod," "Expect Wounds," "Deal with Criticism," "Build Past Failure," and "Sanctify Ambition." If this is where you are living right now, you may wish to read part 4 first, and then come back to the front parts of the book.

Our society needs people exercising spiritual leadership today. Not tomorrow. Not in theory. Not as a slogan. If we do not have multitudes of people exercising spiritual leadership in every area of society, the masses of people will live at the level of animals, going through life guided only by their base instincts and appetites. Is this not what we are seeing today? Whole segments of society aligning themselves with groups, movements, and tribes that have no transcendent principles. Driven by what they want. Energized by nothing more than free-floating anger.

If ever there was a time for spiritual leadership, it is now.

Another major emphasis in this book is the truth that spiritual leadership may—and must—be exercised by followers of Jesus Christ *in every walk of life*. There was a time when spiritual leadership was seen as the prerogative of priests and pastors, CEOs of Christian organizations, and writers of "spiritual" books. But this is to limit spiritual leadership, and everyone loses.

Followers of Christ exercise spiritual leadership whenever and wherever they take the spiritual resources they have in Christ to make a difference in the lives of other people. Some of that will be in the church, but most of it will be outside the church, out in the world and in our families, where we spend most of our time. I hope that this book can be one more signal to our educators and attorneys, doctors and healthcare workers, managers and community leaders, parents and influential friends that you are honoring Christ in your "spiritual leadership" wherever you live. We need to drive that affirmation deeper than ever, and motivate ever-wider groups to see themselves in this way.

Our world is in trouble; our culture is in trouble; we are in trouble. We need armies of people who will rise to the call of God and be powerful influences in their organizations, schools, businesses, churches, and families.

People are looking for wisdom, discernment, power, truth, and other qualities that begin a transformative work on their lives. They need to know that the reigning power of God has come in Jesus and is active in the ongoing work of the Holy Spirit. Just think of the effect if massive numbers of believers woke up to their potential to exercise spiritual influence in the schools where they teach, in the boardrooms where they deliberate, in the clinics where they care for people's health, in the churches where they serve, in the assemblies where they legislate, in the homes where they raise their children.

This is not a book about management or organizational leadership per se. There are plenty of good books on those topics. We will be looking at more personal, core issues. Whether we like it or not, our influence flows directly out of the kind of people we are. This is inevitable.

I had the privilege of serving as a pastor at Elmbrook Church for a thirty-year span, the last ten as senior pastor, and now as minister at large. Over that span I had to learn about leadership in good times, in tough times, and in tragic times. I learned about planning and reacting, creating and repairing. I learned about responding to critical situations, oftentimes unforeseen. While I dealt with thousands of people, multi-million-dollar budgets, and hundreds of leaders, I learned the most from one-on-one interactions in which I saw the miraculous effects of the influence of God.

Oftentimes I learned the most from my disappointments, frustrations, and failures. I hate disappointing others; I hate disappointing God far more. But it seems God allows us to slip and stumble so that when we offer people recovery and redemption, we know something of what we are talking about.

Along the way I learned from leaders I have known in the business community and the medical field. I have also learned from lawyers, educators, community leaders, elected officials, and I have watched how God used small group leaders, children's ministry leaders, missionaries, and so many others in amazing ways. Over the years, I've conversed with, worked with, or interviewed a wide array of influential leaders who are impacting the world or just their own neighborhoods. I suppose in the back of my mind I have a catalog of great leaders I have met, but just as important, I hold on to pictures of great moments of influence and leadership, which may come from almost anybody.

I have taught on the themes of this book in various regions of the world—Latin America, China, India, Europe, Africa, North America—because I wanted to test the ideas in crosscultural settings. That is how we get at core issues, which is where the power is. I believe we need to pursue those principles that are so core to human nature that they transcend country and culture and age. It has been affirming to get the response of seasoned leaders, and invigorating to hear from younger influencers what their dreams are. There are exciting days ahead.

So whether you are an influencer in the marketplace, in a church, in a school, in a small group, or even within your family, I hope you will find encouragement here to apply yourself fully, not to let the disappointments and failures derail you, and to have a deep assurance that God is our leader and we get to be his agents.

HOW TO USE THIS BOOK

Influence is not a solo act. We need each other so that we don't sit on our heels or drive off a cliff. We need to hear each other's stories and bear each other's burdens.

You can read this book on your own, but you will benefit more if you read it with others so you can discuss the ideas and apply them together.

The book is divided into twenty topics covering four main themes, so you could, for instance, work through the book over a four-week period, reading five chapters a week. Rather than do all the reading in one sitting, space the chapters out to have time for reflection. If it takes you twenty minutes to read a chapter, take forty minutes to reflect, pray, take some notes, prepare for a book discussion with your group, and/or add your comments or questions to the online community.

Look for extended resources for this book at *www.theinfluence project.com.*

Part 1

GETTING GROUNDED

Chapter 1

WHY IS SPIRITUAL LEADERSHIP IMPORTANT?

There is a view of leadership today that is disappointingly simplistic: merely getting people to do things. Many are successful in their efforts. They can get people to give money, attend large meetings, vote a certain way, develop a group identity, even to sacrifice. These are good things, but are not the apex of what Christian leaders are called to do.

A higher view of leadership includes higher purposes. This leadership aims at great aspirations, brilliant ideas, and high ideals. It aims at the betterment of people—their character and dignity, not just their pocketbooks and status. It is committed to transformation. This is spiritual leadership—*spiritual* because it is empowered by the Spirit of God and its ends are spiritual vitality and growth. And the amazing thing is that God uses us even in our brokenness and sinfulness to lead people toward this transformation.

Is there any doubt we need wider and deeper spiritual leadership in our world today?

If You Influence Others, You Are a Leader

You may be perusing the opening chapters of this book wondering whether you have a hand in spiritual leadership today, or even whether you are a leader at all. Let's establish this from the outset: if you exercise influence in any way in the lives of other people, whether they are members of your family, participants in your church or organization, workers under your management, students under your teaching, or anyone whom you can influence toward higher purposes—yes, you are a leader.

That is one of the great new developments in spiritual leadership today. People in an ever-wider body are realizing that influence is at the heart of leadership and that spiritual leadership is possible for anyone in any station in life who is able to influence others in the direction of God's character and will.

You do not need a business card and a title to be a leader. You do not need an office. You do not need to be ordained. Far too often Christians have made the mistake of thinking that only pastors or other ordained people are able to exercise spiritual leadership. This is understandable at one level because chaos ensues if everyone thinks he or she should have the authority to direct whole groups of people. But on the other hand, it has been a tragic mistake for the majority of the people to be passive and let a few people take responsibility for all influence and leadership. Our great obligation, according to the teaching of Jesus in the parable of the talents, is to employ all of God's gifts in all of God's people in the service of God's great work to promote restoration to broken people.

In this book we avoid the term *spiritual leader* and instead stick with *spiritual leadership*. As soon as we talk about the spiritual leaders in our world today, we tend to focus on gurus and clerics, everyone from Billy Graham to the Dali Lama to the beloved missionary your church supports, instead of focusing on the multitudes of ordinary men and women who should be exercising spiritual leadership exactly where they are. This is what is needed today. In its strongest forms, leadership is action and movement and response, not fixed roles and statuses. Leadership is when people are moved toward a good end, not when one person grabs a place of privilege.

There are many people called leaders today, but there is a desperate need for leadership that has spiritual substance. The only enduring influence is God, so we must guide people to the place where God does his transforming work. This form of leadership understands God as the influence and we as his instruments. We stand in a kind of nexus where God's power meets human need. The greatest Christian leaders have all lived out of this conviction: that they were not the real influencers, but that they were being used by God, who brings enduring, transforming influence upon people's lives. God is the leader, we are subleaders, and the dividing line between us is not just one step of rank. On one side of the line is Creator; on the other, created. Our best days are when we realize that we get to have a small part in the healing of the world that the Creator has determined he will do. Amazing.

God is the true influence, and we must keep that in the forefront of our thinking at all times because as much as we talk about God, we keep defaulting to ourselves. We love real-world pragmatism—the grease under our fingernails, the blisters on our hands, the sweat on our foreheads. God's Word points us in the direction of spiritual influence and leadership, but we can't wait to build the next machine. If we're wise, we'll realize the necessity for and the limits of pragmatism, because we know what it's like to drive the machine, we've been in the ditch, we've fixed the engine many times over—but we are refreshed when someone reminds us of the real destination over the horizon, and that the purpose of driving is greater than drivenness.

Spiritual Leadership Is About People

Many forms of leadership focus on specific outcomes: increasing the bottom line of your company, getting more members, promoting a specific cause. But in spiritual leadership, people themselves are the matter at hand. People are not a means to an end; they are the end. That's what makes spiritual leadership both challenging and deeply rewarding.

People are complicated, and so the call to influence people for the good is complicated. We have to decide when to tell people what to do and when to teach them principles so *they* can figure out what to do. We have to figure out the goal or destiny of what we are aiming at. In an organization, the goal may be short-term and measurable. In spiritual leadership, the goal is helping people to be restored to that dignity called the image of God—far more difficult to measure, but also far more important than anything else. Spiritual leadership is thus an extension of discipleship. Influencing people toward the restoration of the image of God leads to groups that have more spiritual character and organizations that have something like souls, not just objectives.

Spiritual Leadership Is About Life

Spiritual influence is challenging because it is about life itself. All of life. People need help with their relationships, families, sins, addictions, jobs, money, health, dreams, disappointments, and so it goes. They need to have discipline when things are going well in life, and they need survival techniques when they are in the middle of storms. People want to know in whom they can believe, what they can expect in the future, and whether anyone cares for them—the three big questions of faith, hope, and love. We have the remarkable opportunity to help people flourish, to live that good life that God has defined as good. To help people find wholeness, or *shalom*. Grateful people will look back across the years and say to those who led them to live under God's transforming influence, "Thank you. You made a huge difference in my life. What you said was a turning point for me; what you did brought God's power to bear on my life."

Because spiritual leadership is about life itself, whatever messages we bring to people, we have to live that way ourselves. Like it or not, we are models, even though our lives are far from perfect. People watch how a leader deals with criticism, works through crises, handles personal shortcomings, rises to an opportunity, or descends to help someone hidden.

Gone are the days when people are looking for leaders who seem perfect. Many more people assume that an influencer who is "the real deal" has been through failure as well as success. People want to see perseverance in the face of pain and loss. They want to know how to get out of a bind, deal with discouragement, and conquer one's inner demons.

Spiritual Leadership Is About Values

All people spend their time and energies on the things they value the most. The question is, What are those values, and how do values actually work out in a practical way in people's lives? The same thing applies to organizations, which are just collections of people and reflect their own values systems.

Spiritual influence and leadership are about helping people shape their basic values according to what God values. This is not terribly complicated. We need to value the people we live with and work with. We value people because of the Genesis principle: men and women are created in the image of God (Gen. 1:27) and therefore have a dignity that must be respected and reinforced. Belief in the restoration of dignity shapes everything in your influence and leadership. We also should value the created world because God fashioned the universe as a way of displaying his glory and power.

Spiritual Leadership Is About Character

The philosopher Plato told a fable about a shepherd named Gyges, who one day found a magical golden ring. As he was sitting with friends, he twisted the ring on his finger and became invisible. Twisting it again, he reappeared. It soon occurred to Gyges that he could use the power of the ring to his advantage—going anywhere he wanted to and doing anything without anyone knowing. He moved into the royal court, seduced the queen, murdered the king, and took over the throne. The point of the fable is that we would discover what our true character is if we were invisible, able to act without detection. We find out what kind of people we are by looking at how we behave when no one else can see us.

Spiritual influence is about character—the kind of people we are, the shape of our inner and outer lives. Our word *character* comes from a Greek word which goes back to the word for a stamp that leaves an imprint, like the dies used to make coins. Character is the very shape of one's inner life (thoughts, motives, values, desires), which is revealed in the shape of one's outer life (actions, behaviors, speech, relationships). And because of the power and inevitability of influence, the shape of one's character will be stamped on the character of other people, for good or for ill. Influence is unavoidable. Everyone leaves a mark. The question is, What kind of mark will it be?

Spiritual Leadership Today

In this book we will unpack some of the universal laws of spiritual leadership, looking at the principles and the practices, and seeing where the divine-human nexus makes the decisive difference. We'll look at key biblical texts, as well as stories from history and from today.

Part 1 is called "Getting Grounded." If we desire to have enduring influence and exercise good spiritual leadership, we ourselves need to be grounded in God. That may seem obvious, but let's not pass it over because it is obvious. So in part 1 we look at engaging with God as a way of life, about the meaning of discipleship and following, and about building integrity. Good leadership is built on these foundations.

Part 2, "Taking Initiative" opens up some of the dynamics of spiritual leadership. Our influence comes from discovering, communicating, and reinforcing really great ideas and ideals. These are the seeds that sprout and grow and multiply. We also look here at exploration and opportunity, which are ways in which we break out of the status quo. And we look at how we react to and speak into crises. Those are the moments when we exercise the greatest spiritual leadership.

In part 3, "Going Deep," we look at the special treasures of spiritual leadership like discernment and wisdom. People are influenced all the time by leaders who tell them where to go and what to do, but the deepest form of leadership is when we impart wisdom so that people can figure out for themselves what to do. This really is what most people want. The know they can follow leaders who hold their hands and lead them by their noses, but most people really want to be mature and self-directed. And that, after all, is the only way spiritual influence will be passed on to succeeding generations. In part 3 we also look at three dynamics at the core of influence: power, authority, and truth. Untold wreckage has happened by leaders who abuse power, usurp authority, and twist truth. The distinctive of spiritual leadership with integrity is that it puts people under God's power, and God's authority, and God's truth. It is a tricky business to lead people to the place where they are truly under God's influence—and for us to live there ourselves.

Finally, in part 4, "Facing Challenges," we look at ways we can understand and deal with the expectations people put on us and even those we place on ourselves. We look at how we can persevere and plod ahead when things are truly difficult. We consider the wounding of "friendly fire," dealing with criticism, and building past our failures. And we end by looking at ambition—the kind that can undermine and disqualify leaders, and the way ambition can be sanctified so that we are driven in ways that honor God.

Working with Others

In all this we need to work with each other. We need to work hard to discover our complementary abilities and roles. If you work through the principles of this book with your peers, you will benefit from the insights of others—a skill and commitment the best leaders always cultivate.

You may be a leader-in-training. If so, then this is the time to build on the right foundation. Or you may be a veteran leader and, like so many of us, need the renewal that comes from realigning yourself with the Good Shepherd.

Your work may be in a church, and you sense a need to strengthen or restore the integrity of your spiritual leadership. Or you may work in a business, and you are wondering how you can make spiritual principles and power the distinctive quality of your efforts. If you are an educator or the leader of a nonprofit organization, you will want to ponder how spiritual influence is your opportunity to infuse knowledge in or to restore dignity to the people you are trying to help. If you are an artist, this is an opportunity to connect expression and influence. If you work in government, this may be your opportunity to decide what you believe about social purpose and power.

Wherever you can exert spiritual influence, you will live with a sense of wonder that God allows you—even you—to be part of this.

God has great things he wants to do in this world, and he wants to use ordinary people like us in his work of restoration. The question is, Are we ready to follow him, and only then, to lead?

The Most Influential Person in a Century

For years *Time* magazine has come up with a list of the most influential people of the year. At the end of the twentieth century, *Time* raised the question of who was the most influential person not just of the previous year but of the prior century. When the editorial decision was made, the opinion landed on the German-born Jewish physicist with the signature tousled hair, a man easily recognizable any place in the world, Albert Einstein. He was not a leader of industry or the founder of a movement. He ran no organization. So why did the editors call him the most influential person of the twentiety century?

Because Einstein understood something about the hidden powers of the cosmos, his findings made possible things like nuclear energy, nuclear medicine, and yes, nuclear weapons. It all really went back to when Einstein was just five years old, on a day when his uncle showed him a compass. The boy was captivated by the sight of the needle moving this way and that, pushed as if by magic. As an adult, Einstein spoke about that moment as the time when he realized that "something deeply hidden had to be behind things." Einstein, the Nobel laureate and one of the most famous people in the world in the late twenieth century, spent his life unlocking the hidden power of the physical universe.

There is an analogy here with spiritual influence. Einstein was deemed by *Time* magazine the most influential man of the whole twenieth century, and it was because he unlocked the potential of unseen forces in the realms of what we do see. So it is with spiritual influence and leadership. The believing Christian knows the almighty Father God, the eternal Son who had a hand in the creation of all things and who became human to restore all things, and the Holy Spirit who moves among us today—guiding, empowering, enlightening. The power of the living God exceeds all other powers, including the powerful leaders of governments and industry and societies. In spiritual leadership, we are helping people find and connect with the power and majesty and truth of the almighty God.

What Exactly Is Influence?

A typical dictionary definition of *influence* is "the capacity to have an effect on the character, development, or behavior of someone or something." Notice the internal and external features of influence.

As we carry out the calling of influence, we are appealing to people in the deep part of their lives where opinions and biases are formed, where thoughts germinate, values are shaped, and decisions begin. Influence is a spiritual matter. It takes place at the core of human nature. Influence is the form of leadership that has the best chance of having enduring effects. Accomplishments are good, but it is when they are supported by deep influence that the effects go farther and last longer.

Now, there are those who would argue that the way to influence people is to get them to do things, and that with the passage of time people's minds and hearts get shaped by their patterns of behavior. Action leads to belief. But this contradicts one of the core principles in Jesus' teaching, which is that change happens on the inside and then is expressed on the outside (e.g., Matt. 15:1–20). This was Jesus' revolution against deeply entrenched religious traditions that sought external conformity as obedience to the law of God, without regard for the spirit of the law.

Spiritual influence and leadership take place at the level of the human spirit, and they are prompted by the Spirit of God, who works to reform the human spirit, bringing people back to the shape

God designed in the first place. This happens by the inflow—the influence—of the Spirit. And it happens through a thousand imperceptible steps.

Today influencers and influences abound, whether or not they call themselves leaders. Some are healthy while others are corrupt, greedy, wicked, immoral or amoral, shady, sleazy, unscrupulous. "Leader" is not a qualitative label. Franklin Delano Roosevelt and Adolf Hitler were both brilliant leaders. They influenced with big ideas, captivating words, and persuasive presence. This should be sobering to us, especially because the moniker "spiritual leader" tells us nothing about motives and ends. Some leaders have guided people to summits, and others, off cliffs. For every Billy Graham there has been a Jim Jones, the cult leader who led nine hundred followers into an act of mass suicide in the jungles of Guyana.

Leadership can be dangerous because influence is potent. When we lead, we assume that we have the responsibility to shape other people because we have been handed that responsibility. But often positions of leadership are based on presumption. Why do human beings exert influence over others? Much of the time it is merely because they can. And that is not an adequate reason.

Any good leader will stop occasionally and ask, What gives me the right to influence other people? Where did I get the idea that I'm so smart? Who do I think I am? And then good leaders will look at that compass which pointed him or her in this direction in the first place. A higher order, a purpose, a summons, a calling. Poor leaders will not look for the compass. They don't care about right or wrong, good or bad. They have never looked for a compass, because their forward motion is just a matter of gut and drive and force of will. Leadership that is entirely self-directed will always be pathological. The only thing worse than worshiping idols is to act like an idol.

A good influencer looks at the compass of moral order and realizes, I'm not so smart. I'm not very powerful. And I know I'm not good enough myself to define the good life for someone else. But it appears that I have an opportunity and a calling to dip into a higher wisdom, to try to live it, and to pass on those gifts. That is where the power of spiritual influence begins.

Spiritual influence matters because it touches the essence of what it means to be human and focuses on the issues that matter most in life.

One last point about influence. You might have noticed that in the middle of the word is something like "fluid." We get our English *influence* from the Latin *influentia*, which refers to something that flows in and causes changes, usually a force that is imperceptible or hidden. All of us have forces and powers at work on us and within us, and we can exert force on others to affect the thoughts and actions of others, or even the course of events. We are influenced, and we are influencers. But it takes time and repetition. The force or power of influence usually lies beneath the surface of things. True influence is not tame or subtle. It is the power of change because it goes deep; it keeps streaming; it exerts force.

This is the power and the potential of spiritual leadership today.

Chapter 2

LEARN TO FOLLOW

We cannot all be masters, nor all masters
Cannot be truly follow'd.
— *William Shakespeare, Othello*

The best leaders are the best followers. That's because they have been powerfully influenced by God and by other people and are enthused for others to benefit from what they have received.

Some of the most dangerous leaders are those who think they know better than anyone else, who are interested only in their own inventions, and who relish the isolation of being out ahead of everyone else. Think of it this way: Are you more assured by people who are alone at the leading edge, or by people who are respectful of the accomplishments of those who went before? The best leaders you ever followed did not learn leading by leading, but by following. These follower-leaders don't have the illusion that their best ideas are the ones that no one else has ever had. They value innovation, but that does not mean trashing all prior ideas. Innovation means renewing the best ideas (*innovare*: "renew, make new"). The best leaders make new things happen, knowing that this usually means renewing a classic idea. In contrast, insecure leaders always want others to believe they are the inventors of the brand new. However, many a "brand new" idea has just been stolen from someone else and given a fresh paint job. If we are building on someone else's great idea, why not admit it?

Our paradigm of service, influence, and leadership is rooted in the summons of Jesus: "Follow me." That call is like a clap of thunder in the middle of a clear blue day. The first disciples, who became courageous, remarkable leaders, are the foundation stones of every successive generation of disciples and leaders. They were follower-leaders. When they were naive and unformed, they thought they were in control, but when the Spirit of God filled them, they realized that any authentic influence they would have on others would be the influence of the Spirit. This is the difference between Simon Peter before the resurrection of Jesus, and Peter afterward. Before, he was supremely self-confident in his convictions and commitments—and fell flat on his face. After, he led with conviction and power that he knew came directly from God and might lead anywhere.

Here is where it all began: "As Jesus was walking beside the Sea of Galilee, he saw two brothers, Simon called Peter and his brother Andrew. They were casting a net into the lake, for they were fishermen. 'Come, follow me,' Jesus said, 'and I will send you out to fish for people.' At once they left their nets and followed him" (Matt. 4:18–20).

This "following" took the form of actual physical walking toward and then with Jesus. Feet on the ground, ears attuned, eyes focused on Jesus. Peter and Andrew, James and John, did not sign up for a seminar. They followed—literally. They entered into a relationship with Jesus in which they were fully exposed to both his words and his deeds, twenty-four hours a day. These disciples were formed not only by what they heard but also by what they saw—and by what they touched, smelled, and even tasted, as when Jesus fed the multitude with a few fish and loaves of bread. The taste of bread in their mouths prepared them to understand Jesus as the bread of life, sent from heaven. Years later when the disciples became powerful influencers, when they began a world-changing movement, they were able to look back on a total immersion experience of following Jesus. Even with him physically gone, they were following him more completely than when he had been present with them, because now they knew by the Spirit of God just what following him meant.

This following took the form of listening. But not merely hearing words, writing them down in a notebook, and letting the ideas superficially penetrate the brain. Leadership cannot be packaged in a three-ring binder, and we don't become leaders by progressing through Unit 1, Unit 2, and Unit 3. The listening of Jesus' followers was a process of question and answer, question again and answer again, scratch your head, screw up your face, walk away, watch what he does, come back for more, sleep on it, talk to your colleagues, test it on strangers, raise the question again, taste the truth, hunger for more, leave it alone knowing that there is a banquet to come back to. Jesus didn't put his disciples on an assembly line — he took them on a journey. Listening needs to happen over a lifetime. None of us need to wait to register for the best-in-the-world training seminar that will transform us into effective leaders. The training is under way right now, every day, as we listen like people who strain to hear distant thunder.

This following took the form of engagement. The disciples learned from Jesus by engaging with people, healing them, confronting them, comforting them, sometimes being chased away by them. The disciples sometimes came to town as heroes following the Hero (Matt. 4:25; 15:30; 19:2; 21:9), and sometimes as outcasts entering the den of his enemies. The disciples also followed Jesus when he wiped the dust off his feet and disengaged from people who rejected the message (Luke 9:3–5). Being a spiritual influence includes discerning where you can be effective and where your efforts would be a waste of time.

Follow Me?

Spiritual leadership today means inviting people to follow by listening, watching, and imitating. Not that this is a safe proposition. The easy thing to do is to influence by words alone, perhaps even secretly hoping that no one is really watching who we are behind the words, because we know that our house is not entirely in order, which is a silly thing to do since none of us have our lives entirely in order. All of us are embarrassed by some of what we are. Humility dictates that we shudder to think of people examining our lives and imitating the worst side of our temperaments.

People today want to know whether the talk of their leaders matches the walk. Is there congruence here? Or is the talk just talk? The cry for authenticity is really people saying, "Don't give me a line; I don't care about mottos. I don't need a show; I need reality. Show me the way. Show me that it is trustworthy. Show me that it works. Show me that it rings true. Tell me why I should allow myself to be influenced by you."

Every audience has a baseline of people expecting congruence and authenticity in their leaders. But there are also masses of naive people who can be swayed by the catchy slogan or the satisfaction-guaranteed promise. There are television teachers, traveling evangelists, and marketing geniuses skilled at attracting substantial followings. In this sick, symbiotic relationship, the "leader" offers happiness or health, large numbers of people "follow," and the following feeds the ego of the "leader." Some will authenticate their own message and influence on the basis that a crowd is following them, but the only reason they have a following is that they offered vague promises of contentment or prosperity. Or they get a following merely through personal charisma, that glint of light that draws the eye.

Some claim authority based on numeric results. "More" authenticates. Many people will take numbers alone as validation of leadership. But history shows that not everyone who draws a crowd leads the crowd toward life. Or it can work in the opposite direction: someone claims authority by the exclusiveness of their following and the smallness of the group. A cult's self-definition is centered as much on the masses who do not belong as on those who do.

But when leaders get it right, when they start the day with one singular desire—to follow Jesus wherever he may lead—it is a wonderful thing to behold. Jesus still deploys his disciples into villages and cities to confront sin and defend the underprivileged. Tough times may lie ahead—because that is the way spiritual progress is made—but God's power will prevail, not ours. At the end of the day, it does not matter whether our names and reputations have advanced, but that someone, somewhere gains a clearer view of Jesus.

The greatest gift a leader can pass on is the model of the follower-life. Making people dependent on us today only sets them up for disappointment later. Eventually, people will lose their leaders, because no human leader is steadfast like God. Teaching people to follow Jesus puts people in the one place in the universe where they will never be left alone.

Held Captive

One of the boldest, most strong-headed, even obstinate leaders in history, Martin Luther, was actually radically committed to following. Look closely and you will find a phalanx of prior authorities he followed. A young monk with a deeply troubled conscience, Luther submitted to the orders of his superior mentor, Karl Von Staupitz, that he go to university for years of intensive biblical education. In that experience Luther made a fresh personal discovery of the gospel of grace and knew that he would forever have to subject all his thoughts to that and other core biblical truths. At the general assembly of European lords in 1521, presided over by the Holy Roman Emperor, Luther said, "My conscience is held captive by the Word of God." While his opponents viewed him as bullheaded, arrogant, and intractable, Luther viewed himself as radically submissive. Those who knew him personally found him to be unassuming, approachable, even plain. He married a simple woman, and he presided over a household of six children, six live-in nieces and nephews, and many eager students.

Luther found in the writings of Augustine the same gospel of grace that he discovered in Paul, and so he let Augustine be his teacher. He had no personal ambition that drove him to break from the Catholic Church. He tried to suppress the radical impulses of some of his followers who were tearing down the art in their churches and dismantling all the institutions of the late medieval church. He wanted to follow his tradition as far as Scripture would allow him—he did not want to invent anything. The idea of "reinventing the church" (a phrase we sometimes hear today) would have been nonsensical to Luther. Invention (by Jesus), yes. Reform, yes. Reinvention, no.

Luther was a leader who impacted history—only because he followed people and principles higher than himself. Most important, his absolute conviction about the sovereignty of God meant that he viewed his own leadership as directly and practically derived from God. Luther lived in the divine/human nexus, by temperament, by theology, and by policy. Had he not, he probably would have remained a quivering, guilt-ridden, hidden ascetic—never to be known or named.

Followership Today

Recently, a new word has been used in discussions of management and leadership: *followership*. While the word is not in the English lexicon, it comes up in writings and seminars all the time. Most often *followership* is used to distinguish leaders and followers in an organization. The logic goes something like this: leaders need to understand the role of followers. Know the dynamics of how and why people follow, and you will be a better leader.

Fair enough. But if the discussion stops there, we run the risk of dividing people into two camps: leaders and followers. Instead, we should remember that all people—even leaders—are followers, and that people who don't have a leadership title are oftentimes the linchpins of influence.

A powerful thing happens when leaders don't view themselves in distinction from followers, but see themselves as leader-followers. Consider this: no one really wants to follow you, per se. They really don't. They want to know that, by following you, they are really following a higher principle, a transcendent truth. In spiritual followership, people want to know whether they are being led by and influenced by God. They want and need meaning, redemption, and purpose. These are things no human leader can give. What the leader can do is to live them out and then pass them on. So what does that look like in practical terms?

- It is contributors helping to pay for a building project because they know that it will promote kingdom work.
- It is a midlevel manager knowing that the spiritual principles of the Christian owner of the company are not just words but are the true convictions and lifestyle of the owner.
- It is a teacher in a high school inspiring mutual respect among students by consistently showing respect toward the students.
- It is people listening to a sermon knowing that the preacher's feet are planted firmly in biblical truth, not just personal opinion.
- It is a teenager following the advice of a father who is looking not just for conformity of behavior but for an authentic God-following in his kid.
- It is a church congregation engaging with the surrounding community, not just in a single event, but through ongoing connections.

Do you see why we need armies of influencers today? If you ask people who has been most influential in their lives, they generally will not talk about the authors they've read, the historical figures they've studied, or the pastors they had when growing up. They almost always talk about real people whom they knew personally who poured something directly into their lives. Proximity is the key. We all exercise the greatest influence on the people and organizations that are closest to us. Those relationships are our circles of influence. That is the power of proximity. And it is one more reminder that influence is intensely personal.

Ultimately, the best way leaders can teach people how to be lifetime followers (and then, perhaps, leaders in their own right) is to model dynamic followership. When a leader models collaboration on a project, with energy and commitment and joy, others watching will see the power of people banding together for a common cause. When leaders talk about the new insights they are getting from their reading, they inspire others to be lifelong learners. When a leader shares what he or she has learned from mentors, that encourages others to go looking for their own mentors.

In the end we have nothing to offer people unless we follow Christ ourselves. Jesus set the baseline: "Whoever wants to be my disciple must deny themselves and take up their cross and follow me" (Matt. 16:24). This is our calling. "To this you were called, because Christ suffered for you, leaving you an example, that you should follow in his steps" (1 Peter 2:21).

Chapter 3

ENGAGE WITH GOD

> Whoever believes in me, as the Scripture has said, rivers
> of living water will flow from within them.
>
> —*Jesus*

Several countries in Southeast Asia celebrate the regional new year with a water festival. Traditionally, people sprinkle each other with water as a sign of respect and blessing, but many people intensify it with wild, joyful, boisterous dousing of anybody and everybody with water. Walk or drive down the streets during those days and you might be accosted with garden hoses, water cannons, water pistols, or even bowls and cups filled with water. It is raucous. It is fun. It is vivid. Everyone knows it is out with the old, in with the new.

Water was a key feature of the ancient Jewish festival called the Feast of Tabernacles. For the first seven days of the festival, with trumpets blowing, a priest would take water from the Pool of Siloam and carry it through the streets in a golden vessel, eventually delivering it to the altar in the temple. A rabbinic saying describes the event: "He that never has seen the joy of water-drawing has never in his life seen joy."

Jesus was in Jerusalem during the Feast of Tabernacles when, on the climactic day of the festival, he stood up and shouted out, like a different kind of trumpet: "Let anyone who is thirsty come to me and drink. Whoever believes in me, as the Scripture has said, rivers of living water will flow from within them" (John 7:37–38). The gospel of John then has this explanation: "By this he meant the Spirit, whom those who believed in him were later to receive" (John 7:39).

Remember, influence means something hidden flowing out in order to affect others. Jesus talked about the spiritual reality of a person taking in the life of God and then having "rivers of living water flow from within them." This is a wonderful description of spiritual influence — not the kind of thing you will hear at a leadership training seminar while you sit on an uncomfortable seat at a long table in a hotel somewhere — but perhaps the most important principle you will ever get anywhere to deepen your ability to serve and lead others. You seek the "flowing in" of the truth and life of God, and it flows out to the eternal benefit of others. Amazing. What would happen to the quality of our leadership if we committed ourselves entirely to this dynamic? What if we really believed that we "will be like a well-watered garden, like a spring whose waters never fail" (Isa. 58:11)?

John makes this clear: Jesus was speaking about a spiritual reality that would happen with the coming of the Holy Spirit — the time when God would strategically begin a work in the world and use believers as his instruments.

Spiritual influence is founded on a real connection with God. In that nexus we see people differently, understand their potential and problems differently, and conceive our role as leaders differently. If we really want to help people and have an enduring effect in their lives, we will engage with God.

Use the word *spiritual* and people will hear different things. That should come as no surprise since the word intentionally points us toward what is beyond us, beyond measurement and analysis, beyond a definition in a dictionary. The word *spiritual* reminds us that we are more than bodies, that our work is more than slinging bricks and mortar or tracking spreadsheets, and that God — who is Spirit — is the impetus for all authentic spiritual work.

Made in the image of God, who is Spirit, human beings are by nature spiritual. Spiritual influence means awakening people to the creatures they really are. It is like rousing armies of people who are asleep to a great work they must do.

We have to be careful with the word *spiritual* because it has some- times been used by people wanting to create an elite class of people who have an exclusive relationship with God. Some of the ancient Gnostics taught that people are predetermined to fall into one of three categories: spiritual, soulish, or fleshly. Some people are natu- rally spiritual, others have the potential to rise to that level (soulish), and others are completely hopeless (fleshly). Like a caste system, this understanding promoted an elitism that contradicted everything Scripture says about the potential of all people. In a far subtler way, many people today will distinguish some people who are very "spiri- tual" from ordinary people. But this is not the way things really are.

All people are made in the image of God, with the potential and longing to be spiritually alive. The whole purpose of spiritual leader- ship is to help people connect their spiritual craving with God, and then to be led into a purposeful life mission. There is no human being who is not spiritual.

So what is the biblical idea of "spirit" or "spiritual"? The Hebrew and Greek words in the Old and New Testaments are fairly straight- forward. *Ruach* (the Hebrew) and *pneuma* (the Greek) both mean "wind" or "breath." The words are intentionally sensory. Wind is wild and capable of great power. Breath is the clear evidence of life. Wind and breath: both invisible, both influential.

"The LORD God formed a man from the dust of the ground and breathed into his nostrils the breath of life, and the man became a living being" (Gen. 2:7). These first words about the first Adam are a parallel with the last words formed from the last breath of Jesus, the last Adam: " 'Father, into your hands I commit my spirit.' When he had said this, he breathed his last" (Luke 23:46).

Spiritual, in other words, does not refer to one special subset of human activities. Some think we are spiritual when we go to church, but when we exit the door, we slip back into some lumpy, cloddy existence. But leaders are not spiritual only when they mouth the word *Jesus*. The creation account of Genesis 1 tells us that God created all human beings to be profoundly and irrevocably spiritual. But because people choose to deny their spirituality and disconnect from God, they need spiritual awakening.

Combining the word *spiritual* with *influence* leads us to this important conviction: leaders can fulfill a distinctly higher and better purpose if they link their influence with the work of the Spirit of God and with the spiritual qualities of the people they are working with. This is the hidden power of spiritual influence. It means being who we really are and drawing on God as he really is.

The Horizontal and the Vertical

When we read the Bible we see *Spirit* with a capital *S*, and *spirit* with a lowercase *s*. God the Spirit. Human beings as spirit.

We do not *have* spirits in the way that we have gall bladders and lungs. We *are* spirit. At the core of who we are is that immaterial self, created in the image of God, and thus capable of amazing things like intellect, emotion, will, creativity, morality, and altruism, but also vulnerable to the devastating corruption which turns the spirit toward avarice, violence, malice, self-adulation, and many other corruptions. *Spirit* is what makes human beings uniquely human. So if we as human beings are spiritual creatures, then leadership is a responsibility with immense potential for good — or for harm. Leadership involves spiritual beings influencing other spiritual beings. And thus all leadership is a spiritual matter if it involves moving and motivating human beings. If we affect the choices of others, shape their values, direct toward a mission, develop their minds, and create the environment in which they work with others, then we are dealing with spiritual realities no matter the setting. Genuine spiritual influence is needed in churches, schools, offices, agencies, and families. This is the horizontal dimension of influence.

But the stakes are higher still. The other kind of Spirit is God. As Jesus put it: "God is spirit, and his worshipers must worship in the Spirit and in truth" (John 4:24). Across the centuries of Christian discussion about God, sometimes *Spirit* has highlighted what God is not. God is without form, without matter, without physical dimension or limitation. There is a point to this (called the *via negativa* in the Eastern Orthodox tradition), but it is saying far too little about God. *Spirit* simply describes who God really is. Breath and wind are enormously helpful descriptions of human beings as spiritual creatures and God as the ultimate Spirit. Breath is the marker of life. No breath, no life. Wind is invisible, unpredictable, and can be either gentle or overwhelming.

So there are these two dimensions that make influence spiritual: first, human beings (who are by nature spiritual) influencing other human beings (who are also spiritual); and second, human beings acting on behalf of and with the enabling of the eternal God who is Spirit. These are the horizontal and vertical dimensions of spiritual influence. And where the two converge is the human/divine nexus.

In Real Life

But let's picture this in real-life terms. The horizontal dimension of spiritual influence is when

- an office manager so dignifies the work and the collaboration of employees that the mood of the office adds something to the workers' lives. They leave at the end of the day tired from the work but not worn down as people. The manager leads by adding to people's identity, rather than taking away.
- a teacher starts a new term by beginning to get to know the students as people, taking the appropriate time for this process and not defaulting to stereotypes. The teacher is motivated by a vision to shape lives, not just dump information, pass quotas, and get to the next summer break.
- a community leader sets about to reduce random crime in one city block by cleaning up the environment, removing graffiti, and enlisting neighbors in a neighborhood watch program. The soul of the neighborhood gains dignity.
- a youth leader in a church walks with a student whose mother is battling cancer. The two-year-long struggle ends in pain and ugliness. And the youth leader knows enough to see the day after the funeral as the real beginning of personal ministry.

These are examples of the opportunities we have every day to do something that respects the God-given dignity of people made in the image of God. Dignity is everything. All leaders want to build; good leaders know there is nothing more important than building people.

In real-life terms, the vertical dimension of spiritual influence is when

- a pastor stands up to preach one Sunday when he has been worn down by life circumstances, is feeling spent and uncertain, but puts faith in God and the truth of his Word and experiences the energy of the Spirit in the preaching.
- a Christian counselor hears the horrific story of a teenager who is being abused by a relative, is initially at a complete loss for words, but then finds words of guidance and comfort that come from a supernatural source. She knows that the Spirit of God gave her just the right words at the right time.
- a man admits to a friend that he has had several affairs, and the friend, who is a believer, finds words he never had before to describe both the grace and the judgment of God. He knows God has granted him a word of wisdom. They chart a course forward and lines of accountability.
- a leader of a ministry spends a day in prayer and a whole new paradigm for ministry seemingly pops into his head. In the weeks that follow, in careful discussions, the new direction is tested with others and the idea takes on a life of its own. But it all began in a moment of true inspiration, which may not have happened if the leader had not made space for prayer.

Engaging with God Begins with Bowing

Spiritual leadership begins with worship and prayer. Not just an hour a week when one goes through certain motions with a group of people, but worship and prayer as a life stance and mindset. A life rhythm of worship and prayer reinforces the submission of the self, putting us in a posture where God can use us.

Two words that define worship in the New Testament are *bowing* (literally, to bend the knee) and *serving*.

In ancient times, subjects bowed before kings and other sovereigns as a way of acknowledging a relationship of submission. Believers take that stance—happily—before God, the beneficent king. Bowing to the greatness and goodness of God is the wisest thing any person can do.

Prayer and worship continually reinforce our essential position in the cosmos. There we are—sons and daughters of Adam and Eve and sons and daughters of God. Higher than the beasts, lower than God. Grotesque and dangerous when we are disconnected from our creator, noble and powerful when we draw our life from God. When we sing praise, we adore; but if we choose not to adore our creator we cut ourselves off from the life of God. When we live a pattern of prayer, we live in the nexus, practicing the biblical reality that we can live with God, for God, by God, under God. When we open ourselves up to the truth of the Word of God, our minds are widened as we gain a higher perspective on almost every issue of life. It is like climbing a mountain and looking across the landscape, finally understanding the whole and seeing every feature for how it fits in the whole. When we submit to God, we forget about our small-minded concerns, our biases, and our preferences.

An attitude of bowing helps to ground us as leaders, equipping us to manage *some* things because we know that God is master of *all* things. Prayer and worship set the entire posture of spiritual influence.

Engaging with God Means Serving

The second word for worship in the New Testament, *latreuo*, means "to serve." Recently there has been a renewed interest in what is sometimes called "servant leadership" (spelled out by Robert Greenleaf in his influential book *Servant Leadership: A Journey into the Nature of Legitimate Power and Greatness*). Throughout the ages many leaders—political, military, business, media—have exercised influence over others in order to get something. From simple profit to theft and domination, people are driven to try to control other people. Servant leadership turns that on its head. Servanthood is a response to a true sense of calling to give more than get. We need constant reminders of this as Christian leaders because the "get" motive is always right there with the "give" motive. None of us is ever entirely free of that hungry little troll in us that is always asking, "What's in it for me?"

The problem is that being a leader often benefits the leader, even if he or she is acting in the name of God. We must be ruthlessly honest about this. The allure of leadership may include financial gain, success, preferential treatment, status. Even a morsel of flattery tastes like a piece of rich chocolate. We need to continually check our motives because the temptations all people experience are multiplied many times over for people with influence.

To make matters worse, leadership status can seem to offer a special kind of righteousness. Spiritual pride is certainly the most destructive temptation of all, because it contradicts the message of grace and the mission of spiritual influence. We may rightfully gain a sense of satisfaction and accomplishment as we serve and influence and lead, but we must not cross the line into a sense of being specially favored by God for our achievements.

Spiritual pride and self-righteousness don't rise up in us as big noisy monsters. Rather, they whisper in our ear that we're shining, that people are noticing us, that we're better than others. And then, hooked on the feeling, we have to keep feeding it, telling ourselves all along that our motives are pure. Like addicts who are always trying to sustain the buzz, leaders become obsessed with status. When that line is crossed, we have ceased being servants. We have killed the prospect for authentic spiritual leadership. The powers of darkness need no more complicated tactic to corrupt spiritual leadership than small addictive doses of adrenaline and spiritual pride.

Perhaps this is why Scripture doesn't have a generic word for leadership. The concept of leadership is not unbiblical, but all leadership forms in the New Testament have specific applications. There is little interest in a generic form of leadership.

Who Is Greatest?

Jesus shut them up. They had been walking to the town of Capernaum, some pairs and clusters of disciples talking along the way. One conversation got heated and turned into an argument. The disciples probably tried to keep their voices down, but that did not prevent Jesus from overhearing the exchange. After they arrived at their destination, Jesus asked what they were arguing about on the road. Silence. Not a word. The gospel of Mark tells us, "They kept quiet because on the way they had argued about who was the greatest" (9:34).

What Jesus next said needs to be stamped on our minds. Jesus gathered the Twelve, had them all sit down, and started with: "Anyone who wants to be first must be the very last, and the servant of all" (Mark 9:35).

If leaders across the ages had obeyed this one command of Jesus, the world would be in a different place. If thousands of influencers today acted out of a true servant spirit and really took the position of being the very last, then the world would see not weakness, but the power, authority, and truth of God coming through the words and work of those leaders. When we shove our way to the front, we do not display the glory of God. We obscure it.

God will advance whom he wants to advance. People are smart. They can distinguish between those who push their way into the spotlight versus those who find themselves—surprised, bemused, even embarrassed—to be within the field of light God is shining. Spotlights are for singling out performers on a stage. But God uses light to make visible everything and everybody, and good leaders point people not to themselves, but to a vivid world of God's creating.

Jesus had a single message that he proclaimed, a principle which handily sorts out all our bumbling attempts at influence and leadership. The kingdom of God has come. In Christ, God has shown his hidden power and authority. God has changed the rules of the way the world works. He has changed the standards for leaders. Now actions that appear to be small are the authentic beginning of the greatest deeds—like a tree sprouting from a tiny seed. Now we know that influence works like yeast in a lump of dough. Again, it is hidden. But it pervades. It infiltrates. It rises. Jesus takes a small group of men of average intelligence and status and makes them the follower-leaders who would change the world. A message that seems foolish is the height of wisdom.

All authentic forms of Christian leadership are connected to Jesus' message of the kingdom of God.

Devoted

A young man stands in front of a painting by Domenico Feti titled *Ecce Homo* ("Behold, the Man") in a museum in Dusseldorf. In it Jesus looks down, head tilted, the crown of thorns pressed on his head. The inscription on the painting reads, "This have I done for you. Now what will you do for me?" The young man is caught up in the mystery of the truth, sensing Christ speaking directly to him.

He was born into one of the noblest and most powerful families in Europe and grew up in a magnificent castle in Dresden, Germany. But his whole life he used his wealth and privilege in the service of Christ. Count Nicholas Ludwig von Zinzendorf showed signs of a remarkable relationship with Christ from his earliest years. At the age of six he talked with Christ as a friend for hours a day. "A thousand times," he said, "I heard him speak in my heart, and saw him with the eye of faith." His sense of identity came from Christ, not from his lineage. He said, "Of all the qualities of Christ the greatest is his nobility; and of all the noble ideas in the world, the noblest is the idea that the Creator should die for His children."

As a young man he was torn by his vocational options: study for the ministry or take his position as count. When he was in his teens, he formed a secret society with other young men of the noble class. The purpose of the Order of the Grain of Mustard Seed was for these young people in the privileged class to use their power and influence for God's purposes.

In 1722 a group of Moravians sought his permission to live on his lands, which was the beginning of a settlement called Herrnhut, "the Lord's Watch." Zinzendorf was of a kindred spirit with the Moravians in their deep, heartfelt devotion to God and a conviction about the mission Christ gave his followers. This radical new community became the base for sending out the earliest Protestant missionaries, initially to slave populations in the West Indies, and eventually influencing Africa, America, Russia, and other regions. The work expanded throughout Zinzendorf's life, including a visit to America to do mission work among Native Americans.

The outstanding feature of Zinzendorf's life was his deep devotion to Christ. He was a man engaged with God. He emphasized the spiritual vitality of the inner life but did not limit it to himself.

And out of that came enormous influence. His spirit spilled out in missionary enterprises and was influential in other major movements, like the Methodist revival under John and Charles Wesley. Zinzendorf's faith had a powerful missional direction issuing from a profound personal engagement with God. Here is a principle all of us can take away: before we can help others, we have to enrich our personal relationship with God. That is where the power is. That is where the power will always be.

Today's God-Engagement

Examples of extraordinary devotion raise many issues for spiritual influence today. Are the Zinzendorfs of the world the norm for Christian leadership, or special instances of God anointing specific people for specific purposes at specific times? The question can be answered by the biblical teaching about the filling of the Holy Spirit. On the one hand, it appears that the Holy Spirit does unique works at pivotal times in history—usually unanticipated by believers, and always exceeding the church's expectations. On the other hand, everyone who has a hand in spiritual leadership must assume that engagement with God is the norm and the base of their leadership. No one should stand around waiting for the next Zinzendorf or Bonhoeffer or Graham. Spiritual influence is for this day—and God uses millions of no-name influencers every day in the simplest selfless acts of service. They are the teachers whose names will never be in the newspaper, pastors who will never author a book, managers who will never be profiled in a magazine, artists whose work is buried in layers of collaboration, writers whose sphere of influence is a few dozen people who read their blogs. But they are the army that makes things happen. To them devotion is its own reward. For them influence is a continual act of giving, nothing more complicated than that.

Today ever-larger numbers of people want their leaders authentically engaged with God. They are less impressed with showmanship, and downright skeptical of public figures whose lives seem too good to be true. More and more people want God-engagement in their leaders because that is what they themselves long for.

So our marching orders seem straightforward: use every means possible to be grounded in God, because the only enduring influence we have to offer others is the influence God has in our lives.

Chapter 4

BUILD INTEGRITY

If you have integrity, nothing else matters. If you don't have integrity, nothing else matters.

—*Alan K. Simpson*

The highest currency leaders trade on is trust. If there is trust between leaders and those they lead, any reasonable goal is attainable. Without trust even the simplest objective is a hill too high to climb.

We need a deep understanding of where trust comes from, because trust does not happen simply by asking for it. Acceptance may be free, but trust must be earned. And the earning begins when there is integrity in the life of the leader.

When we think about integrity, attributes like honesty, humility, and right motives come to mind. This, however, is a pretty tall order, particularly given the reality that all of us are broken, flawed, damaged, sinful creatures. People who exercise good spiritual influence begin with the assumption that they have no inherent right to demand or expect trust from anybody. They do not assume people respect them; they seek to earn others' respect.

Jesus once gave his disciples a picture of two men praying at the temple. One was a Pharisee who fasted twice a week, gave away a tenth of his money, and thanked God that he was better than other men. The second was a very worldly man who beat his breast saying, "God, have mercy on me, a sinner." The second man went home right with God, Jesus said. The operative principle: "For all those who exalt themselves will be humbled, and those who humble themselves will be exalted" (Luke 14:11).

Yet when people size us up, we are given to strutting and crowing and bragging. We don't begin where Isaiah began: "Woe to me!... I am a man of unclean lips" (Isa. 6:5). Or where Simon Peter began: "Go away from me, Lord; I am a sinful man!" (Luke 5:8). Among all the prophets and apostles, the most major of the major prophets (Isaiah) and the preeminent representative of the followers of Jesus (Simon Peter) both began at the same place.

So integrity begins with the conviction that we do not have it. Aspiring leaders must not entertain the slightest temptation to posture as flawless, complete, inerrant. Leaders do not have credibility because of personal holiness, but because God has consecrated the leader for God's own holy purposes.

Once we admit our lack of integrity, God begins to build something new and solid — a new life rebuilt with the broken stones of a prior life. Simon Peter the fisherman knew what it was to watch a building arise from the brokenness of personal failure. Jesus named him *Petros*, Rock, but only later did Peter understand that God restores broken stones and makes them integral to (i.e., having integrity with) his great construction project. "As you come to him, the living Stone — rejected by humans but chosen by God and precious to him — *you also, like living stones, are being built into a spiritual house to be a holy priesthood*, offering spiritual sacrifices acceptable to God through Jesus Christ.... But you are a chosen people, a royal priesthood, a holy nation, God's special possession, that you may declare the praises of him who called you out of darkness into his wonderful light" (1 Peter 2:4–5, 9, emphasis added).

What Is Integrity?

Integritas (Latin) means "whole or intact." An integer is a whole number like 3, 7, or 10. No fractions, no divisions, no ambiguity. Integrity is a state of being or becoming whole, sound, consistent, connected. Engineers and architects use "integrity" to describe well-designed buildings, bridges, and towers that will not fall down because the spans of steel, layers of concrete, bolts and screws, glass and silicone work together to create stability and strength. But engineering integrity also includes flexibility. A skyscraper crudely built with rigid material is certain to crack the first time a ground tremor happens. If you've ever been at the top floor of a major skyscraper and felt like it was moving a little with gusts of wind—it probably was. Integrity, in other words, is not just a matter of building something bulky and stiff, but building something that can flex and bend.

Is it not true that the strongest (and most effective) leaders also choose to flex when that is what discernment dictates? Wise leaders make plans, but retain flexibility. The book of James warns us about being rigid in our "schemes" of planning (James 4:13–16). Wise leaders put people together into groups and organizations, but remember that people are not like the gears of a machine and need to be led as the free agents they are.

The New Testament uses the analogy of a building, a "spiritual house" that is built with "living stones," in the words of 1 Peter. Spiritual influence does not begin with building organizations or institutions, but with building people and communities. And if those communities lead logically and necessarily to organizations and institutions, so be it. But even then the integrity of the work is determined by the construction that happens at the core human level. Great universities, churches, and benevolent organizations derive their greatness from the person-by-person integrity of building lives and of bringing "living stones" in contact with each other until a "spiritual house" is built.

So if a leader is convinced, "I need to have integrity; I want to build integrity in my life," how does that happen? We tend to think that integrity means avoiding the big, ugly stuff: no robbery, no sexual scandal, no cocaine use. But looking for disqualifying characteristics is only the crudest way of thinking of integrity. Integrity is both a quality of life and a process of living. It is a commitment to a whole-life process of constructing and reconstructing character, all with a background of humility in which the leader acknowledges just how far he or she falls short. Integrity is a process that is never finished.

The pursuit of integrity includes a growing coherence between public and private life. An influencer who is one person in public and a completely different person in private is leading a disjointed life. If public persona contradicts private personhood, then there is a danger, in a worst-case scenario, that private corruption is being masked by the image of public life. It is almost too painful to recount how many times across the ages leaders have ridden a wave of public ascendancy and influence, all the while hiding a complete lack of character. Sometimes the farce is exposed, and oftentimes not.

Coherence of public and private does not mean that a leader can have no private life or that honesty and transparency require that every detail of his or her private life be announced in public. Everyone needs a private life, and the fine details of personal struggles need to be shared with appropriate circles of confidants. For all the complexities of balancing privacy and openness, the basic principle remains the same: those in positions of spiritual leadership cannot be one person in public and an entirely different person in private.

Integrity also means coherence within one's personality. Lack of integrity occurs when a person splits belief from behavior or intellect from will. It is the split person who can preach against sexual immorality while carrying on serial affairs. Crises of integrity grab the headlines, but here is a frightening thought: a leader can be divided in far subtler and less scandalous ways, but have just as profound a lack of integrity. Greed is hard to quantify, but it has seriously compromised the integrity of many leaders. Greed can dress itself in the pious clothing of "vision" and "passion." But when greed is the driving energy of leadership, purer motives are choked out. Jesus warned us that one cannot serve God and mammon at the same time, because he knew that we will sacrifice our integrity in the process. Divided allegiances on these matters amount to no allegiance. Leaders who split who they are at the core of their personality are living in a continual crisis of integrity, and it is only a matter of time before everything falls apart.

Paul outlines a definition of integrity in his list of qualifications for elders. Strictly speaking, the list is for church officers, but it serves as a picture of spiritual integrity for all leaders. "Now the overseer is to be above reproach, faithful to his wife, temperate, self-controlled, respectable, hospitable, able to teach, not given to drunkenness, not violent but gentle, nor quarrelsome, not a lover of money. He must manage his own family well.... He must not be a recent convert.... He must also have a good reputation with outsiders, so that he will not fall into disgrace and into the devil's trap" (1 Tim. 3:3–7).

A few main themes are repeated in this list: the importance of self-control, healthy relationships, and a good reputation. No one possesses these qualities absolutely, and there is no scriptural "passing grade" defined. Rather, these characteristics paint an overall picture of integrity.

Integrity does not mean sinlessness. David was a far-from-perfect man, called by God to do one simple thing: be a shepherd of his people. What he did with his skills was coherent with who he was in his heart. "And David shepherded them with integrity of heart; with skillful hands he led them" (Ps. 78:72). Here are two sides of spiritual leadership: integrity and skill. Skills may give us success, but integrity makes enduring influence possible.

Advancing While Holding On to Integrity

John of Antioch was a preacher in the cosmopolitan capital city of Syria in the late fourth century. He became the most powerful Christian leader of his day when he was recruited by Roman Emperor Arcadius and his wife, Eudoxia, to become the leader of the church of Constantinople (modern Istanbul). As archbishop he was the most influential leader of the most influential city (with some contention from Alexandria and Rome). But in the end John of Antioch was removed from his office, exiled from the city, and marched to his death—all because he would not compromise his integrity.

He was recruited to the archbishopric of Constantinople—almost kidnapped really—as imperial guards showed up one day in Antioch announcing that the emperor was summoning him to the high seat of Constantinople. John was already widely known as the best preacher of his time. People thronged to hear his sermons and regularly interrupted them with applause. (In one sermon John chastised his listeners for their distracting applause, but did it so eloquently, he elicited more applause.) His method was unusual for his time—a verse-by-verse elucidation of the original meaning of the biblical text, applied in ethics and morals to everyday life. People jammed into the church in order to hear him.

As archbishop of Constantinople, one of the most important Christian centers of the day, John preached in the great church there. But he did not play by the rules of power and prestige. He had lived the ascetic life early on, and carried with him core convictions about simplicity, modesty, and pure faith. Upon arriving in Constantinople, he sold the fine dinnerware of his predecessors and gave the proceeds to the poor. He wore simple clothing. He saw people at his residence when there was good reason to, but never for social showmanship. He did not play political games by trying to get in the good graces of the emperor and empress. And when he believed there was reason to confront the behaviors and policies of powerful people—including the emperor and empress—he did not hesitate.

The people didn't know until it was too late the day the imperial guard arrested John and whisked him out the back door of the cathedral and to a boat that took him away to exile. When it was discovered, a riot broke out in the city and someone set the cathedral on fire. John was returned to his post some weeks later, but his own sense of integrity compelled him to pick up his prophetic teaching where he left off. Sensing impending doom he preached (with reference to Empress Eudoxia), "Again Salome dances, again she asks for the head of John on a platter." The next exile drove him deep into the wilderness, where he eventually was overtaken by exposure and fever and died.

How many of us, if recruited to the highest position of influence and spiritual power, and given complete access to the most power-ful political leaders of the day, could and would resist the tempta-tions of privilege and self-importance? Would we have the courage to speak out in the face of injustice? Would we reject all the perks of superstardom?

John took with him to the chair of Constantinople the things that he learned in the wilderness of Antioch. A later age called him John Chrysostom ("golden mouth") because of his eloquence. In his own day, he thought of himself as a simple servant.

Today's Challenges

The core issues of integrity remain the same across the ages and across cultures. The coherence of the person, the consistency between the public self and the private self, the need for sound character—all lie at the heart of spiritual influence.

But today we face special challenges to integrity. First, more masks are available today for us to use to fool the public. Facebook and Twitter make it possible for a person of influence to appear more open and transparent, but really hide behind an image easy to construct and manipulate with a camera and a computer keyboard. We can become like the Wizard of Oz, hiding behind a curtain, manipulating a machine that produces awe, but is just so many props.

Then there is the more widespread brokenness of our social structures. Leaders frequently need to carry on despite deep troubles in their own families. Moral confusion, addiction, and alienation within the family are frequently the backdrop of a leader's personal life. Some surmise that they need to step out of leadership in order to care for personal needs, but oftentimes the right thing to do is to keep at the work, knowing that there are no guarantees of peace and contentment in this life. Many leaders face powerful spiritual opposition. In business a leader's rivals are other businesses. In spiritual leadership the rival is something immense, powerful, and malicious—evil itself. Commerce concerns itself with competition; spiritual leadership is a state of war.

All of us are affected by the brokenness in our world. The incidence of depression and despondency is alarming. Sometimes the reason is that a leader, coming from a broken home and a series of broken relationships, is working out of an unrecognized deficit in his or her own life. And in other cases, leaders repeat unhealthy patterns that they see in the governing structures of the country they live in. Often our Christian leaders don't behave any better than our corrupt political leaders; they just repeat the same patterns.

And then there is this pathology: competition. People of influence have always compared themselves to each other—just look at the tensions between leaders in the New Testament churches. To be out ahead of others gives us a sense of power and status. But today this need to compete has been magnified many times over. With our enhanced communications we can track almost everything, and so many leaders have chosen to define spiritual success in the language of statistics, a principle that is hard to reconcile with Jesus' theology of the kingdom of God, which defies all measurement.

Often what really fuels crass competition among leaders is a psychological drive. In a broken world and a broken society and within broken psyches, we have a desperate need to justify our own existence. Power and position are central temptations for leaders—but today we also have the simple psychological need to feel validated. We may preach a gospel of unmerited favor, and then in the next breath couch everything about our leadership in terms of merit. Why do leaders do that? To what degree does the pathology of competition rise out of personal pride or its antithesis, personal insecurity? Why do we not see the infection when leaders act out of wounded or inflated egos? Why don't we see that when we are driven by a spirit of competition, we spoil the very work we are trying to accomplish? Why aren't we embarrassed before God?

On a more positive note, the public can help filter out leaders who have no integrity and give the stage and the microphone to people who don't lust for them. Younger people today are not as impressed with style and rhetoric. They want the real deal. They expect spiritual influencers who are congruent in their public and private lives. In fact, it would be a good thing if people rose up and demanded integrity in their leaders. This is the power of ordinary people: they can reinforce the principle of integrity by following leaders who value it; and they can choose to reject leaders who flaunt power and mock integrity.

"May integrity and uprightness protect me, because my hope, LORD, is in you" (Ps. 25:21).

In this opening section of this book we have looked at "getting grounded." In the first chapter we looked at the meaning of influence. Any of us who are in a position to be an influence in the lives of others need to heed the call to leadership. The world is in such great trouble. We need leadership that goes deep to the core issues of people and their organizations. Spiritual influence is the hidden power behind leadership—the sustained influx of great ideas, solid wisdom, reliable truth. Influence is not merely persuasion or salesmanship but a spiritual dynamic that shapes our thinking and being. Our influence in the lives of others must always have a grounding in God.

In the second chapter we looked at learning to follow. The best leaders are the best followers. They scour the earth for good, wise, reliable ideas. They follow the model of Jesus' followers, who, after becoming leaders, became more radically committed to following Jesus than ever before.

Third, we looked at engaging with God. Spiritual leadership is founded on an attitude of prayer and worship—submission *to* God, and willing service *for* God.

Finally, in the fourth chapter we looked at the need for integrity. Leaders need to seek wholeness in their lives: a congruence, a connectedness, a consistency. This is easy to say, but difficult to accomplish, because of the brokenness of life. Integrity begins by admitting that we have none. Only God is able to take our confused, conflicted, broken lives and put things together. But he does do that, making it possible for us to model a longing for integrity that surpasses a longing for influence. And then authentic influence can begin.

The preparation for spiritual leadership does not begin with acquiring skills. For example, we know next to nothing about the several years that the apostle Paul lived in Arabia before he began his public, world-changing ministry. They were silent years. But it is safe to assume that the most important thing that happened during those years is that Paul was "getting grounded."

And then he was ready to take initiative.

Part 2

TAKING INITIATIVE

Chapter 5

EXPLORE NEW HORIZONS

Exploration is really the essence of the human spirit.
—*Frank Borman*

The most expansive, energetic force in the world today is the Spirit of God. More than a message, more than a creed, and more than a plan, the Spirit of God is like an unrelenting mighty wind driving across the oceans, propelling us toward previously undiscovered countries. And so leaders cannot stand in one place. They cannot get to a certain status and then lock in what seems to be at that moment a good thing. Spiritual influence means continual movement, a continual exploration of new horizons.

This principle is both global and personal. Jesus charged all his followers and those who were follower-leaders to be propelled out of Jerusalem (home territory), into Judea (regional influence) and Samaria (crossing into foreign soil), and to the uttermost parts of the world (the universe of humankind itself). And so Christian leadership in its healthiest and bravest form is an expansive mission at one level tracked by distances charted on a world map, but at another level counted one person at a time. We are called to deal with the dregs of human suffering, the whirlpools of intellectual dilemmas, and the outer space of lostness. None of it is easy.

This mission is intensely personal. The trajectory toward the uttermost parts of the earth begins with the next simple step that we take, by meeting people we have never met before, going to places we have never been to before, creating ministry that we have not engaged in before. But true exploration, made possible by solid faith and courage, is how we find the leading edge of the kingdom of God.

People Will Follow Explorers

Everyone wants to discover something new and fresh. Discovery is intriguing and invigorating. Discovery reminds us that our lives are not over yet, that there is more to life than what we can see right now, and that any of us may have yet-undiscovered potential.

Discovery-leading is telling people that you, the influencer, are driven by a conviction that something new is around the corner and that others can join in the quest. You don't even fully know what it is yet, but you know the direction is right, light is spilling over the horizon ahead, and no one has yet arrived at the final destination. Leaders don't motivate people by their knowledge of the future, but by their anticipation of what is possible.

Discovery-leading could be

- a mission organization crossing into a new country previously thought out of bounds.
- a small group committing to sponsor a refugee family.
- a business leader partnering with a local social cause and redefining growth in both spiritual and economic terms.
- a small business leader with expertise in job training joining a central city church in order to address unemployment in that area.
- a church deciding to divide into three new churches instead of building a bigger facility.

Some leaders believe that they must always project a concrete vision of the future and define the vision in detail; but spiritual leadership is often most effective when people are drawn into a vision not yet fully formed, so they get to be part of the discovery. People do not want to be herded like cattle. They want to be fellow explorers.

So, for example, one person has a burden for the profound needs of a refugee population in his city. He starts to talk with others about the need, and the burden gradually becomes a vision in his mind. Not a vision with details and how-to's, but a mental picture of the grace of God flowing to the refugee group through many possible mercy initiatives. He shares that vision with a broader base of people, asking, "What do you think?" Two things happen: others begin to see the same need and sense the same burden; and they contribute specific ideas: What about education needs? job placement? housing? a church plant? They brainstorm about possible resources: funding, expertise, networks of similar work, key leaders, constituencies who would have an interest. Gradually a plan emerges. It is just a one-year plan, not a ten-year plan, because the leaders see this as an exploration with many unforeseen challenges and opportunities. In the first year a couple dozen people are involved, but in the second and third year a couple hundred people sign on, and a nonprofit organization is founded to carry on the work. Four years in and the organization has discovered three main ways to help the refugee group and has discarded five efforts that were dead-end roads. They regularly interact with a network of similar enterprises around the country, and their experiences help shape other organizations. Though they have established best practices, they still keep an attitude of discovery about the work, knowing that God may have new horizons for them that they would never come up with on their own.

Plunging Ahead in Faith

Abraham did not know what God's promise of making him a great nation would mean, especially on the day of his death when the only progeny he had was one son and the only land he owned was the patch of ground where he buried his wife.

The exiles returning from Babylon to Israel during the reign of the Persians had no idea how they would rebuild a whole nation, especially when they were surrounded by people who wanted them to fail.

After the crucifixion, Jesus' disciples had no idea how they would find the strength or the direction to carry on without him.

The apostle Paul traveled thousands of miles on foot, horseback, and ship in four great journeys, planting new churches wherever the soil was right. The historical account mentions no list of cities, no particular timetable, and no metrics of success. Receptive Thessalonica and resistant Athens were both valid for the agenda.

Yet in every case, the answers came to the discoverer-followers as they took one step of faith after another, convinced that their mission was not defined by their strategic plans, but by the One who was leading the way.

Do we believe that God's vision for us going forward far exceeds any vision we might have come up with on our own?

You Never Know Where Discovery Will Lead

In 1804 an expedition commissioned by President Thomas Jefferson set out on one of the greatest voyages of discovery in American history. At that time the known regions of the United States were limited to the geography east of the Mississippi — less than a third of the land mass of US territory. What lay to the west, all the way to the Pacific Ocean, was a vast unknown region. The charge given to Meriwether Lewis and William Clark and a few dozen men under their charge was to forge their way west, looking for a water passage all the way to the Pacific for the purpose of commerce.

Eighteen months later, the expedition had failed in that objective. There was, in fact, no waterway connecting the east and west coasts of the continent.

That is the thing about discovery: you may not find what you expected, but what you end up discovering exceeds all expectations.

The men of the Lewis and Clark expedition were the first citizens of the newly formed country to see the vast plains and to experience their beauty and loneliness, searing heat and savage winter. They were the first to approach the Rocky Mountain range and struggle to cross it, and the first to reach the great Pacific Ocean.

How many times they must have wondered how they could possibly describe what they witnessed to their friends and families and to the government officials to whom they were responsible. Would they even be believed? They discovered 179 previously undocumented species of plants and trees. They encountered not five or ten new tribal groups, but forty-seven, including the Pawnees, the Teton Sioux, the Cheyenne, the Tillamook. And then there were the 122 unknown species of animals, fish, and birds. Lewis and Clark tried their best to describe the grizzly bear, the coyote, the harbor seal, the steelhead trout, the prong antelope, the elk—all unknown to people back East. What the Lewis and Clark expedition discovered was not about trade and triumph, but about the land itself. They set out to discover a means of commerce; they discovered something so much more important.

People will be inspired if they hear the conviction that there is a vastness in God—his nature, his ways, his work done, and his work under way—yet to be discovered. We are explorers. We have to alter our maps along the way because our vision of reality has been limited and distorted. And we get to journey beyond the edges of our maps. That takes faith—a lot of faith. Cartographers in ages past drew great monsters on their maps in the uncharted seas, a reminder that going to the edge of the map is where we confront our greatest fears.

Discovery is risk. Not just organizational risk, but personal risk.

Killing Discovery

Often we blunt this drive to discover with questions and doubts and fears. What will a new initiative cost, both personally and in resources? Will the message be rejected? Will the method fail? Will people recruited to the task find it satisfying or disappointing? Will a new thrust outward feel like the Hebrew liberation from slavery, like the weariness of the wilderness, or like the entrance into the Promised Land? Will anyone find milk and honey there, or will it seem like another barren wilderness?

There are numerous things that will kill discovery, among them:

Fear of failure. True discovery requires that we hold loosely any presuppositions we have about what constitutes success or failure. The Lewis and Clark expedition was a failure if defined by its central objective of finding a trade route to the West. But the expedition ended up with far richer discoveries than they ever could have imagined.

Fear of loss. We may be too hesitant to try new models for our work because we don't want to risk losing something that is working now.

Limited objectives. A trip is defined by getting from point A to point B—a quest is so much more. It is mission in motion. A search for what is beyond the eyes. Vision as a revelation of reality rather than a paint-by-numbers canvas. If our stated objectives aim only at what we can see ahead, then we will never lead people into undiscovered territory.

Lack of curiosity. No leader ever discovered something new or created something innovative without the intellectual and spiritual hunger of curiosity. Apathetic leaders produce uncaring followers and detached results. Curiosity is a particular form of passion, an instinct that says, "There is more out there, I know there is. God is on the loose, and if I look with eyes of faith I will be able to see what he wants to do in the world. Every person is interesting in some way." We should be curious about every movement of the Spirit of God—not just the one we are invested in.

Committing to Exploration

A drive to discover can be the engine of spiritual leadership. Sometimes it takes the form of an expedition—the mobilizing of large numbers of people to go on a multiyear quest. But discovery can happen as an everyday experience as well. Discovery does not need a budget, and it does not need to wait for committee approval.

In the next twenty-four hours, or at least in the next week or month, any of us can find some place of discovery that is nearby and does not take months of preparation:

- Read Scripture daily and register one new or renewed insight each reading.
- Meet another leader outside the circles you normally move in.
- Go to a needy place you've never visited before—whether it is in the next neighborhood or another part of the world. But be prepared to give up preconceptions of the spiritual or physical poverty you think you will find there, and look for the grace of God. Be open to discovering your own spiritual poverty.

- Visit a place of refuge and linger there — a hospital, nursing facility, rescue mission, storefront ministry, hospice.
- Mentor a struggling coworker.
- Volunteer to lead a risky project.
- Do something you have never done before. Take a temporary chaplaincy role, spend a weekend with an urban ministry, lead a Bible study in a prison, offer counsel to a couple about to be married, offer to arbitrate a dispute, tutor at-risk kids, be a mentor to someone in a substance-abuse program.

We all must know our comfort zones so that we can stretch beyond them. However, do not seek discomfort for its own sake, and certainly do not try to be some kind of hero. Another way of saying "go beyond your comfort zone" is "discover the undiscovered." Once we leave behind the familiar we will start to see the work God is already doing. And then, in the divine/human nexus, God will wonderfully co-opt us to work where we previously would not have imagined.

She is a nurse and a grandmother and a proper English lady. She always thought her contribution to society would be medical care and teaching. But when in 1982 Prime Minister Margaret Thatcher appointed her a lifetime member of the House of Lords, Baroness Caroline Cox began an astonishing life journey.

The helicopter she was riding in was crippled by gunfire from the ground in a remote territory of Azerbaijan, but somehow managed to make a soft landing in snow. It was her first trip to Nagorno Karabakh in 1992. Baroness Cox (who says, "call me Caroline") crossed militarized borders to get there, where a massacre of Armenians had occurred. The ethnic cleansing left decapitated and burned bodies, kidnapped women and children, homes burned to the ground. It was a risky visit. Yet Caroline Cox returned to the small region, accessible only by helicopter, no less than fifty-eight more times in the years that followed.

She has also traveled dozens of times to Sudan, and to North Korea, Burma, Nigeria, Indonesia, and elsewhere. Her first foray after becoming a member of the House of Lords was into communist

Poland, riding thirty-two-ton cargo trucks delivering supplies. She frequently travels secretly, knowing that the governments of the countries she is visiting do not want her there.

As a member of the House of Lords, she could have settled into the red leather seats of the dignified chambers of parliament, into committees and debates and social events. But her philosophy—derived directly from her spiritual convictions—has always been that advocates for the suffering and dispossessed must go and witness firsthand. To be able to say, "I've been there; I've seen; I know how it is." The people she visits in hidden corners of suffering say, "Thank you for coming. Tell the world what is happening to us."

It has been a journey of faith, which she characterizes not so much as having a long-range plan as walking through doorways that open up. Her efforts have benefited orphans in Russia, persecuted Christians in Sudan, disabled people around the world, and many others. She believes "dignity is a crown of thorns."

Baroness Cox's spiritual influence is expressed through the organization she founded, Humanitarian Aid Relief Trust, and through the many other organizations she participates in. But in the end it is her spirit that has made the impact. Everyone sits up and takes notice of the grandmother of ten, called by some "the battling baroness." But none of it would have happened if she had not been willing to explore beyond her own borders.

Chapter 6

STREAM IDEAS

Great minds discuss ideas; average minds discuss events;
small minds discuss people.   —*Anonymous*

Try this: close your eyes, and for the next thirty seconds do not think about a pink elephant. Remember, you are not to think of a pink elephant. Ready, set, go.

How far did you make it? And what does that tell you about the way the mind works?

One of the most powerful influences in our lives is invisible, sometimes very small, often hypothetical. Ideas. They fill our minds, they motivate our actions. They shape how we view reality and— very importantly— possible new realities. Ideas are sometimes mental impressions and other times full-bore convictions. When connected with creativity, ideas are a flow we call imagination— sometimes a trickle, other times a torrent. People get carried away with their imaginations, which is often the way the best new things happen.

Some leaders say they are more about action than ideas. But unless someone is acting out of pure animal instinct with no thought behind it at all, every action has some idea behind it.

Ideas are at the core of spiritual leadership. They are powerful realities that move invisibly from one person to another. Ideas come in and go out. They get planted and grow. They change and develop. It is almost like they have a life of their own. Every leader should always be asking himself or herself, What are the very best ideas I can flow to others? Or ask this question: Is there one big idea God has influenced me with that ought to be the big idea I pass on to others?

Ideas are mental constructs; ideals are ideas that are so excellent, so perfect, that we will put our lives and reputations on the line for them. The motive for spiritual influence is that we understand good ideas and ideals as gifts from God that must be shared.

One of the most loving things God does for us is to shape our minds with his ideas. God influences us with a steady stream of pictures of reality and transcendent conceptions. God's ideas include the truth about human nature—unique and glorious, broken and wounded, morally perceptive and morally corrupt. God-ideas include realities about who God is: his goodness, greatness, love, holiness. God streams ideas into our minds that are bigger than our minds. No wonder we talk about some things that are so big they "blow our minds."

The Power of Ideas

The action film *Inception* uses a science fiction idea to tell the story of an amazing heist. A corporate spy and thief has developed a unique capability to enter the subconscious of victims while they are in a chemically induced deep dream state, then insert characters and situations into the dream, leading ultimately to uncovering valuable corporate information. The main point of the story turns out to be the unintended consequences of planting ideas in people's minds. When the main character places one idea in his own wife's mind—that maybe the world we live in is just an illusion—the idea takes root, becomes all-absorbing, and ultimately leads to ruin.

Think of the powerful forces in history that were simply ideas before they entered into human experience. Until the moment the detonator was tripped in a metal sphere on a hundred-foot-high platform in the desert of New Mexico on July 16, 1945, the atom bomb was a theory. Just an idea. But in a split second of blinding light and concussion the idea became a force that would make nations cower and change geopolitical realities irrevocably. Democracy was a theory that was debated in the cities of ancient Greece before anybody thought to see if it could work. Long before the Wright brothers flew the first manned airplane at Kitty Hawk, someone had the idea of the airfoil—a wing that would create suction on the topside, making it possible to lift a heavier-than-air machine into the sky. In 1982 a worldwide network of interconnected networks was standardized—the internet—but only on the basis of the idea of "packet-switched networks," which came out of the 1960s.

Then there are the great social ideas: freedom and equality; justice and law; economic opportunity and higher education. Any real-life experience of such things has been possible only because of the ideas behind them. Such ideas do not hang in the air and drop on unsuspecting individuals—people take the good ideas (and bad ones too) and become champions of those ideas. That is powerful influence.

Various biblical authors make clear that our lives must be governed by higher principles. Call them "truth" or "wisdom" or even "rightness" (justice), ideals matter because the best of life on earth is an impress of the God of heaven. Out of those ideals flow ideas. From the structure and substance of our ideas flow our priorities, decisions, and actions. And what we do in life then flows out and influences the people around us. Ideas matter. Great ideals propel us toward open highways; really bad ideas put us in the ditch.

Great Ideas Require Deep Thinking

Spiritual influence gets below the surface of things, and that necessitates dealing with the deeper rational dimensions of issues and ideas. If our thinking is shallow, our solutions will be shallow. All it takes to think deeply about issues is time and effort to look, probe, study, discuss, and research the matters we deal with—all that based on a conviction that making rational connections at a deep level is the way to effect enduring change. Deep thought is more a matter of hard work than of genius.

Some critics of faith think that people who want to be more "spiritual" can only do so by sacrificing their intelligence. These critics understand spirituality as a choice to be anti-intellectual. They cannot understand how anyone would prefer the vague and ethereal to the empirical and scientific. But if all human beings are spiritual because they have been made in the image of God who is Spirit, then spirit will never be set against thought and rationality. Instead, spirit is the apex of mind and order. Being smart doesn't make us closer to God; but being closer to God will energize our minds and create a hunger to find rational connections for all of life.

People committed to spiritual influence should be the smartest people around because they know that the mind is an extraordinary gift of the Creator, whose mind surpasses all other minds. And they are enthused about and committed to the growth of understanding. They see life experience and education, research and simple reading as the way they feed their hungry souls.

In the aftermath of poor leadership decisions, a chorus of voices cries, "What were they thinking?" The truth is, the decision makers may not have been thinking at all. People with no wit and no wisdom are placed in positions of significant influence all the time. That is how we end up with profoundly irrational conditions: monstrous national debt, impulsive business decisions, church ministries detached from all biblical grounding, and a thousand other variations.

We need good ideas, but so much more than the latest best ideas from experts. We need the ideas no human could ever think of. We need the God-ideas about human purpose and dignity, of community and industry, of order and shalom.

Starving the Mind

There are powerful cultural currents today that undermine and devalue deep thought. To begin with, our impatience and desire for the quick fix make deep thought unattractive. It takes too much time, too much effort. We don't have margin for conversations or deliberation. We like short-form reading, and feel so overwhelmed by the number of books available on any topic that we may be tempted not to commit to long-form reading. Piles of coal make us forget there are diamonds out there to be found if we look hard.

We spend less time reflecting on what we read and watch because there is always another channel to turn to, another website to land on. We are like fish darting from one shiny object to the next.

The blessing of the vast body of information available to us is also a curse because it is chopped up into bite-sized pieces. It is also scattered in containers that hold vast quantities of digitized thought. Our reporting of knowledge today does not have the discipline required by printed books and journals. String a few words together—email them, blog them, or tweet them—and you're on the record. And someone thousands of miles away may consider your words as authoritative as someone who has spent a lifetime accumulating expertise. Today anyone can be a publisher. There are upsides to the democratization of opinion—where a blogger's views are as accessible as those of a columnist in the *New York Times*. But credibility is often ignored. The blogger's comments about a country on the other side of the world are not balanced against those of a career journalist who has lived in that country.

This is not a harangue, and it is not a criticism of the tools of mass communication. Tools are just tools. Radio, and then television, and now the internet, are amazing tools. They are vehicles conveying massive loads of intellectual cargo. But we must steer the vehicles, not just passively go along for a ride.

The mind is hungry. But what will be its diet?

Thought and the Image of God

Our capacity for rational thought is central to our dignity as creatures made in the image of God. If we want to honor God by exercising spiritual influence, we will take the time and effort to think deeply about every decision we make. How can we presume to influence others unless we have rational reasons behind our influence?

The Bible teaches that the mind—the capacity for rational thought and deliberation—is an expression of our God-likeness. This is the image of God in humanity. Thought is not separate from other ways we function, like feeling and will, but we depend on the mind to bring truth and structure to our lives. The mind is capable of knowing God, but it is also capable of being corrupted and set against God. The "fleshly mind" is hostile to God and has no interest in submitting to God (Rom. 8:7). There are spiritual forces that blind people's minds (2 Cor. 4:4). Some teachers and leaders influence others out of minds that are fleshly, depraved, or corrupt (Col. 2:18; 1 Tim. 6:5; 2 Tim. 3:8; Titus 1:15).

The mind must be renewed. This is an essential principle of spiritual influence. "Do not conform to the pattern of this world, but be transformed by the renewing of your mind. Then you will be able to test and approve what God's will is" (Rom. 12:2). The mind is only as good as its connection with the God who created it. The spiritually renewed mind goes beyond human will to divine will. The transformed mind is essential equipment for leading any person, any group, or any organization along a trajectory that reclaims their God-created dignity.

Streaming Ideas

Important ideas are the driving engine of progress, the invisible structure behind the things we build. They are also the substance of spiritual influence.

If influence is something that flows in and causes change, a force that is imperceptible or hidden, then ideas are like a network of underground streams that are continually flowing into us and flowing out of us in ways that affect others. Great leadership is based on great ideas and great ideals. But we need to understand how ideas work.

In his book *Where Good Ideas Come From*, Steven Johnson challenges the stereotype of the lone genius in whose mind brilliant ideas arrive full-form. In his study of science, discovery, and innovation, Johnson shows that some of the greatest ideas are the result of mistakes and diversions. He also describes a process he calls the "slow hunch" in which a great idea, sometimes a revolutionary idea, only gradually emerges and is recognized as a great idea through social connections. Johnson also describes how different people will have partial ideas which, when connected, merge into fully formed concepts. The ongoing information and communication revolutions of the twenty-first century give an opportunity for partially great ideas to find other partial ideas and to coalesce into exciting innovation. The implication for leadership is that we need to keep all networks alive and active so that our partial ideas can combine with other ideas and emerge as truly influential forces. Our ideas are always looking to find mates.

However, chaos can break out if we are not careful about the ideas we choose to assimilate and use to influence the lives of others. So we must begin with a core of ideals found in the Bible, which is the framework for rational faith. We must absorb the great narrative arc of Scripture, which goes from creation to fall to redemption to glory. We must champion the great ideals that are rooted in God's own nature, like justice and love.

We live in a time of an incredible flow of ideas — some terrible, and others life-giving. We can stand by passively and assimilate the ideas that flow our way. Or we can work at choosing what we read, what conversations we have, what conferences we attend, and what networks we tie into. Leaders often make the mistake of choosing the conduits of ideas that others impose. If others are "successful" because they read "those" particular authors and attend "that" conference and belong to "those" associations, then perhaps we ought to as well. But a more courageous approach is to make our own choices. Leaders who think outside the boxes other leaders live in will discover truly fresh ideas and introduce them into the flow. They will float the truly innovative concepts, the ones that sound crazy and unrealistic. They will influence because they believe there is gold to be mined, and they are not hesitant about swinging the pick.

Idea Method

A man opens a letter sent to him by one of the great leaders of his day, John Wesley. What would the hero of the Methodist movement have to say to him? The man — who happened to be a pastor — must have withered as Wesley confronted him for having a shallow ministry based on shallow thinking. "I scarce ever knew a preacher read so little. And perhaps, by neglecting it, have lost the taste for it. Hence your talent in preaching does not increase. It is just the same as it was seven years ago. It is lively, but not deep; there is little variety; there is no compass of thought. Reading only can supply this, with meditation and daily prayer.... O begin! Fix some part of every day for private exercise. You may acquire the taste which you have not: what is tedious at first, will afterward be pleasant.... Do justice to your own soul; give it time and means to grow. Do not starve yourself any longer."

John Wesley was a pragmatist. He was the driving force behind a small-group movement; social initiatives from education to health care to poverty relief; and a renewal of church leaders. He rode tens of thousands of miles on horseback in order to preach to hundreds of small clusters of people in villages across England. He was, as we would put it today, a "very busy man."

Yet he recognized that unless he kept learning, and unless there was a cultivated rationality behind all his efforts, his zeal would be like a flash of gunpowder in an open field. As it turned out, the movement he led had a pervasive and lasting effect in eighteenth-century England. Some historians claim that England was spared a bloody revolution like what happened in France because of the effectiveness of the Methodist renewal.

There was careful thought behind the small-group structure called the class system. Wesley's social reforms were based on a strategy that was both practical and biblical. His thousands of sermons were profound in content, but understandable to the masses. We need only picture Wesley holding a book in his hands while riding his horse to understand that Wesley believed his action needed energy—and that energy was in the ideas inscribed by the prophets and apostles, and by contemporary thinkers.

Wesley was not the most brilliant theologian of his day, and he had his share of failures, including a very troubled marriage. But the combination of devotion, personal discipline, and action-oriented ministry makes Wesley one of the best examples of spiritual influence in recent centuries. He thought through every step of his work, because he chose to continually feed his mind.

Planting the Seminal Idea

When we think of the great leaders of the past, we may remember their accomplishments, but just as likely we remember some great idea—a seminal idea—which dominated their lives and drove them to accomplish the great thing. *Seminal,* from the Latin word for seed, means something so compelling that it has a profound influence on others. The seminal idea sprouts and grows, and then it bears fruit. It gives life. The seminal idea spreads its own seed in hidden places. It infiltrates. It may subvert. It has the potential to prevail.

Martin Luther King Jr.'s seminal idea was that all people are owed the same respect because they have the same God-given dignity. Abraham Lincoln was compelled by the seminal idea that the union of the states could not be broken. Winston Churchill championed the seminal idea that tyranny should not be tolerated under any circumstances.

The fourth-century bishop and theologian Augustine of Hippo was later called "the doctor of grace" because he stood against the works righteousness that was taking over many churches of his day. Augustine did not see himself as inventing that idea, but as passing along a principle core to the gospel of the New Testament. Eleven centuries after Augustine, Martin Luther gave voice to the same seminal idea, making his emphasis the free gift of a right relationship with God through Christ.

Closer to our own time, Billy Graham preached to millions of people, delivering the same seminal idea: God's forgiving love in Christ is available to all. John Stott traveled the world planting the seminal idea that faithful biblical teaching is what preserves orthodox Christian faith. Robert Pierce founded the humanitarian organization World Vision on the seminal idea that Christian faith requires a practical response to the physical sufferings of people in the world.

Has God placed a central conviction, a seminal idea in you that ought to be the substance and force of your influence in the lives of others? Some leaders know what their seminal idea is. Others are looking for it. Of course, God may give any one person more than one big idea or ideal. But as a practical matter leaders do need to figure out how to have focus in what they do. And if there is one compelling idea—a burning passion, an ache, a driving conviction, a picture of a better world you cannot get out of your mind—then perhaps that is a seminal idea God has called you to.

Making Space for Idea Growth

So how do we go about deepening the thoughtfulness in our leadership, no matter the setting? And how do we promote intellectual integrity and growth among the people we work with? This is not a matter of IQ, but of choice and discipline.

1. *Take time to think things through.* Pace the decision-making process. None of us want someone to say to us years down the road, "What could you have possibly been thinking?"—and not have a good answer. Sometimes we need to slow things down. Take an appropriate amount of time to discuss, deliberate, research, seek precedents in other leadership settings, study Scripture, pray. We need to be decisive, but we also have to be deliberative.

2. *Read. Read regularly. Read widely. Reread.* A universe of ideas is available to us, and there are two different methods of accessing those ideas. One method is to go looking for a solution when you have a problem. So, for instance, the leader looks for a book on solving office conflicts when a meltdown seems imminent. The better approach is when we continually store up insights and ideas through a regular discipline of reading quality content. This is the way to go. It's like stocking a lumberyard for building projects yet to be conceived. If you do not have a natural hunger for learning, start small. Set a pattern of reading fifteen minutes a day, then gradually increase the time. Perhaps try listening to audio books, which allows multitasking and has a pace that enables you to think through what you are learning.

3. *Broaden your learning.* We also must make sure we are not in a reading ghetto. We all have our favorite types of reading and our favorite authors. But thinking deeply goes hand in hand with thinking widely. All leaders benefit from the lessons of history, for instance. Writings that have stood the test of time are often more helpful than the latest faddish book. We are always tempted by the

promise of the brand-new secret solution. In a technical field it may be necessary to be on top of the latest findings, but in spiritual leadership we need to find and assimilate the principles and practices that have been developed by amazing, intelligent, wise, and godly people—whether the publication date is this year, ten years ago, or a few centuries ago.

4. Learn through other media—but look for quality content. The quantity of audio and video media content is expanding exponentially. We can waste our time on a lot of junk, but if we look hard, we can find excellent content.

5. Be in continual conversation with peers. "Networking" is what we call it today—a great concept that emphasizes connection and relationship. Great ideas we discover will be amplified many times over when we discuss them with others. Through discussion we come to understand the many facets of a really great idea, and partial ideas find each other and emerge as powerful forces.

There is one more high motivation for thinking deeply. In the end, thinking is an act of love. We need to care enough about the people we are serving to do the work of researching, examining, comparing, contemplating, discussing, and testing the best thinking that is flowing past us like a river every day. And thinking is an act of love toward God: "Love the LORD your God with all your heart and with all your soul and with all your mind" (Matt. 22:37). When we think deeply about our leadership values and decisions, we honor and love God, and that may be the most important thing other people witness.

Chapter 7

SEIZE OPPORTUNITIES

A pessimist sees the difficulty in every opportunity; an
optimist sees the opportunity in every difficulty.
— *Winston Churchill*

Spiritual leadership is active, probing, curious, courageous, exploratory. It means taking initiative, but unlike other forms of leadership, the goals and purposes derive from God's own leading. Opportunities abound. There are endless initiatives we may take — the question is what initiatives we *should* take. How does one discern the difference between opportunities God is opening up and opportunities that are diversions from what we should be doing?

The passive approach is: wait to see what comes your way. The aggressive approach is: make your own way. There is another possibility: obediently follow God's way.

If the temptation of the bullish influencer is to knock down one wall after another, the temptation of more passive people is to dawdle and procrastinate in the name of waiting for the Spirit of God. Following God's way is not the leisurely way; it is harder work than the bullish way.

Seizing opportunities is directly tied to the spiritual gift of discernment. When we see what looks like an opportunity, we have to discern whether we are seeing a true opening or just our own wishful thinking or a random idea. Many leaders have walked into walls that their mind's eye told them were doorways. And other leaders have hesitated and let an opportunity pass because they took it as a window to gaze through rather than a doorway to step through.

The word *opportunity* comes from two roots in Latin: *ob* (toward), and *portus* (port or harbor). Opportunity means coming into harbor. That place that is seasonable, suitable, and fit. Where we belong. What makes sense. When we see the right opportunity before us and set our direction toward it, it is like steering our ship home.

Opportunity is not just about what is possible, but what is right. Spiritual discernment of God-given opportunities spells the difference between success and failure, but frequently the decision-making process is challenging. For example:

- Someone approaches you to become a partner in a new initiative. The work looks valuable, the objectives are honorable. But does that mean this is the time and place to make a significant commitment?
- Someone in your church discovers a new tract of land being sold at a bargain price, and suggests it is time to move the church out of a declining urban setting into the wide-open spaces of farmland on the outskirts of town.
- You need to hire for a vacant position. Before the opening is even made public, a seemingly perfect candidate shows interest. You think this must be God's leading because the person almost dropped out of the sky. But is it the right choice or merely the easy choice?
- An evangelistic ministry approaches you about doing a big campaign in your organization. They have an excellent track record of doing this well, but is it the right thing for your organization at this time?
- You feel stale in the work you have been doing for quite a few years. Someone approaches you about a high-level position in an exciting new organization. A change of scenery sounds good; the position would be a career advancement. But you

worry that if you take the new thing, it is more an act of running from problems than of stepping into the right position.

- You didn't expect to be unmarried at your age. You question whether you have had standards that are too high. A friendship seems to be turning into something romantic, but this is not the kind of person you ever envisioned marrying.

How do we decide what open door to walk through?

Finding the Doors

The apostles understood one thing profoundly: they were not the influencers—the Spirit of God was. Peter learned that through failure and restoration. James learned it from the struggles of being the leader of the mother church in Jerusalem. Paul understood it because he was dramatically redirected from being an enemy of Christ to being his ambassador. He brought with him all the tools of his Hebrew education and the status he had as a Roman citizen, but left behind the spiritual pride and self-sufficiency that came with being a Pharisee.

One night Paul was on the deck of a merchant ship pitching in a Mediterranean storm. Would this end up like the last time when the ship was wrecked on a shoal? Would he make it to Rome where he believed great opportunities lay? He was a passenger who had no goods to sell and no fortune to invest. It was just a traveling companion and himself. And they didn't know how they would be received or where they would be living six months later.

The small congregations of Jews spread throughout the Mediterranean world were waiting for Messiah; Paul had the ministry and message about the death and resurrection of Jesus. To Paul, one ripe opportunity after the other were laid out like stepping-stones across a whole empire.

Sometimes the message was received with enthusiasm and gratitude; other times the rejection was severe and even life threatening. Yet when Paul faced severe opposition, he never concluded he had gone down the wrong path or misread an opportunity. Whether the result of the mission was a large number of new believers or virtually nothing (as in Athens), Paul's approach was to keep walking toward the doors.

We can learn a lot from the metaphor of the doorway, as used in Scripture.

Paul says in 2 Corinthians 2:12, "I went to Troas to preach the gospel of Christ and found that the Lord had opened a door for me." He was on his third missionary journey, skipping from one city to the next. At this point, escaping persecution in Greece, he felt "compelled by the Spirit" to get to Jerusalem, though he (rightly) sensed severe trouble ahead. Opportunities are doorways that God opens. It is divine leading, even though you may not be able to predict what lies beyond.

From prison Paul writes a letter, asking believers to pray "that God may open a door for our message, so that we may proclaim the mystery of Christ, for which I am in chains" (Col. 4:3). The man sitting in prison in Rome is looking for a door to swing open. Not the iron gate of the prison, but the doorway of access to people of influence in Rome. Paul was not elitist, but it did not escape his notice that his incarceration had delivered him to Caesar's doorstep. And what might happen if those kinds of doors began to open up (Phil. 4:22)?

One of the greatest doors God opened up in the first generation of believers was the opening of the good news of Jesus to the wide world. When Paul and his companions arrived in Antioch, where the mission journey had begun, "they gathered the church together and reported all that God had done through them and how he had opened a door of faith to the Gentiles" (Acts 14:27). A revolution was under way. It literally changed the world. And the turning point was when God opened a door that only God could. It took a miracle in the human heart for Gentiles to pay heed to, and then to actually believe, the truth that a universal savior for the world had come, and he was a poor Jewish man, living in Palestine, executed as a criminal.

And then there are the "open door" words in the book of Revelation. The vision of Jesus saying to one church, "I have placed before you an open door that no one can shut" (Rev. 3:8). And the famous "I stand at the door and knock. If anyone hears my voice and opens the door, I will come in and eat with that person, and they with me" (Rev. 3:20). Here again, God is in control of opening doors, and he summons us through the doorways he puts before us.

The lesson of the doorway is that we are to look for the opportunities God has placed before us, not just any direction we might forge. So we don't force opportunities, nor do we wait around passively for God to put us where we should be. Like Paul on his missionary journeys, we are to move, probe, explore, watch. When we see light spilling through a crack in a door, if it appears to be God's doing, we run toward it. We "make the most of every opportunity" (Col. 4:5; Eph. 5:16).

Sizing Up Opportunities

How can we know when a God-given opportunity is opening up before us? Here are some signs:

1. Does the opportunity line up with your values as a believer and/or the values of the group or organization you are part of? Good decisions are not ultimately based on tactics or strategy, but on a good value system that underlies the tactics and strategies. And from a spiritual perspective, values are not our arbitrary decisions. We must value some things because God has placed value on them. Value is objective. At the start of all things, God made a value judgment about everything he made: "It is good," "It is good," "It is very good." So when we size up an opportunity, we are essentially asking, "Does God look at this thing as good?"

2. Is the opportunity consistent with your objectives? This assumes we already have a carefully formed idea of our purposes (personally or organizationally). Most of the time we ought to decline opportunities that have nothing to do with our purposes—unless this is God's way of redirecting us.

3. Is the opportunity God's way of redirecting your purposes and objectives? This makes spiritual leadership different from other forms of leadership. When we are in control, we decide our objectives, and we respond to opportunities as we wish. But those who believe they work under the sovereign and benevolent superintendence of the

Creator of the universe assume that there will come a time when they are asked to change their assumptions, their objectives, and their prior trajectory. Abram was told to leave Haran. Moses was told to make an exodus from Egypt. Saul of Tarsus zealously protected the tenets of Pharisaism before being radically redirected into a belief in Jesus. Any of us at any time could be called by God to do something different from what we had been expecting.

4. Does the opportunity line up with biblical values? Some people want to find a biblical reference to line up with every decision they make on the assumption that being faithful to scriptural truth means that there is a chapter and verse for everything we do. But Scripture never says Scripture is prescriptive for every eventuality of life. There are no verses specifically telling us to take a job in a different city. No passage will tell Susan that Mike is the man she ought to marry. Biblical passages should not be used as the rationale to grow an organization. Scriptural truth gives us principles and values, and then we have to apply spiritual discernment in making decisions.

5. Does the opportunity violate biblical values? This filter is very important. It will prevent a believer from taking a job in a movie production company that produces pornography, and will prevent a Christian executive from making unethical moves to squeeze out a competitor.

6. If the opportunity requires the movement of a whole group or community, can the leader convince the group that this is a good direction? Here is another delicate issue for spiritual leadership. On the one hand, if God is opening a door of opportunity, the leader has to call it that. But we all know of times when someone claimed God's leading, but it was imaginary or manipulative rhetoric just to get people to go along. Our protection from arbitrariness comes in the form of deliberation and counsel. Only insecure leaders leap out of the gate and impose on others a full redirection with no process at all. God may give a vision to a singular leader (in fact, vision is ordinarily an experience of the individual), but wise influencers are willing for the vision to be tested by reasonable forms of deliberation. Watch out for the leader who puts a major new idea on the table and immediately forces it to test loyalty or obedience.

Sooner or later every one of us will look into the rearview mirror and have the pang of regret from missed opportunities. Most of the time what's done is done. But we can learn from those experiences — figure out what happened. Did we just not see it? Did we let someone talk us out of it? Did we have a lack of energy or commitment?

But we also have to learn from mistakes — the passageways that seemed like opportunities at the time, but were really wishful thinking or someone else's agenda. Again, we can't change the past, and we shouldn't be paralyzed by regret.

Seeing opportunities with clarity, and then seizing opportunities, is part of maturing. What we can trust is this: as long as we live, more opportunities will lie ahead. But influencers also must pause occasionally and check out their personal approach to direction and opportunity. At the start of this chapter, we contrasted the bullish leader who breaks down doors with the passive leader who just waits for things to happen. These tendencies are usually rooted in our temperaments. They can be directed toward the good — if we are self-aware. We need engaging, active leaders; and we need careful, reflective leaders. Though their personalities may clash sometimes, clearly God intends to get the job done by working with people of contrasting temperaments. And our best safeguard against our personal limitations is to believe, with conviction, that God really is out there going ahead of us, determining directions and redirections and pointing us toward our proper harbors.

Chapter 8

MAKE THINGS RIGHT

At his best, man is the noblest of all animals; separated from law and justice he is the worst.

—Aristotle

If you walked the streets of Berlin in early May of 1945, you may have felt like you were striding a thin line between earth and hell. Smoldering fires, piles of bricks where neoclassical buildings once stood, silence and desolation except perhaps for the sound of a Soviet tank patrolling a nearby street or the barking of a hungry dog. The Battle of Berlin was over. The last of 363 Allied bombing raids over the city complete. Hitler's charred body would soon be discovered outside his bunker. And you may have wondered to yourself, What now? What can anyone do with this devastated world? It is challenging enough to think of what it would take to rebuild the apartments and civic buildings, the museums and churches, but harder still is the question, How can anyone rebuild humanity after its periodic spasms of evil?

The world tried to recover from the disease and the destruction of Nazism while it rebuilt collapsed cities. But a mere sixteen years later the Soviets built a wall in Berlin that demonstrated that history is sometimes a process of swinging from one evil to another. In its turn the Berlin Wall was torn down twenty-eight years later, chiseled apart, pieces sold for souvenirs, and a new generation would have its turn at saying, What do we do now?

Who Can Rebuild?

At this very moment any of us can look around and ask the same question: Who is going to rebuild this world? In the face of economic distress, extreme poverty, human trafficking, moral compromise, government corruption, and personal transgression, who has the courage to do something? To do anything? Is the world simply a lost cause? Is my family a lost cause? The office where I work? The school where I teach? The church where I serve?

No one person can solve the problems of a country, much less the world, but any person at any time can do something. That is a compelling reason to commit to being a spiritual influence. The call of God to the people of God includes this: do what you can—wherever you can—to make things right.

The prophets of the Old Testament brought a message meant to simultaneously devastate pride and restore hope. Their message was this: it is never too late to turn back. God has not given up on the human race, so people should not give up on it either. We are powerless to build or rebuild human life—not just because human problems are so enormous, but because we never had the power to create or restore life in the first place. But God does use us as his instruments to make things right.

Things need to be made right in every arena of life. Educators can convey knowledge that cultivates life. Business owners can open opportunities for gainful employment. Medical professionals can bring physical comfort or healing. Parents can model to their children a life lived right. Government workers can strive for policies that serve and protect their fellow citizens. Some people have a calling to go to far places to do the work of justice. But when we just stand where we are and look around, we will see in every direction opportunities to make things right.

The prophet Micah made a simple statement that challenges us to make things right as God empowers us.

He has shown you, O mortal, what is good.
   And what does the LORD require of you?
To act justly and to love mercy
   and to walk humbly with your God.

—Micah 6:8

We come back again and again to this simple statement because it answers two ageless questions: What is good? What does God want?

This punchy proposition says that there is no mystery about ultimate good and what pleases God, so we have clarity and certainty and focus. Three things: do justice; love mercy; walk humbly. Three things that are really one redemptive spiritual movement: make things right (do justice) as acts of benevolence (love mercy) in the power of God (walk humbly). We memorize this verse not just because it is memorable, but because it summarizes the ethic of both Old and New Testaments. It holds together justice and love, which we so often separate. It joins strong action with humble attitude. It requires submission to God before all altruistic acts. It keeps influence in the divine/human nexus.

Righteousness and Justice

The vocabulary of faith in Scripture includes these fundamental ideals: righteousness and justice. These are not separate realities; they are bound to each other. Righteousness is when things are "right"; justice is how things get set "right." It is all about being right, or getting right while living in a world that is wrong. So wrong. In so many ways wrong. It is also about being wise enough to realize the problem is not "out there," but resides in and emanates from human nature.

A London newspaper one day posed a philosophical question to its readers: "What is wrong with the world?" The brilliant writer G. K. Chesterton sent a letter to the editor:

Dear Sirs:
   I am.

                          Sincerely yours,
                          G. K. Chesterton

"Righteous" people are simply people who are "right" with God. They were estranged from God, sometimes hostile toward God, other times indifferent toward God, and now—by God's grace alone—they have a restored relationship with God. Our broken friendship has been restored (reconciliation). Like convicted criminals we have been acquitted in a courtroom (justification). Like slaves we have been given freedom (redemption). We are like orphans who have been taken in by a loving family (adoption). We are sinners who need the kind of forgiveness that can only be won by a sacrifice of ultimate value (atonement).

Righteousness is not a halo that appears over our heads because we have cultivated virtue or are simply behaving ourselves. Righteousness, according to most biblical scholars, is not a personal attribute at all—it is the spiritual state of a real relationship with God.

And in this is a most amazing spiritual power. People who become right with God have the desire, the calling, and the power to make things right with other people. This is the spiritual logic of justice. God's act of restoring rightness *in* human beings carries through to acts of righteousness and justice *between* human beings. This is true spiritual influence—righteousness flows *to* us, and then it can flow *from* us.

The mandate to make things right is repeated many times in the Old Testament.

> This is what the LORD Almighty said: "Administer true justice; show mercy and compassion to one another. Do not oppress the widow or the fatherless, the foreigner or the poor. Do not plot evil against each other." —*Zechariah 7:9–10*

> This is what the LORD says: Do what is just and right. Rescue from the hand of the oppressor the one who has been robbed. Do no wrong or violence to the foreigner, the fatherless or the widow, and do not shed innocent blood in this place. —*Jeremiah 22:3*

> The LORD loves righteousness and justice; the earth is full of his unfailing love. —*Psalm 33:5*

Just pause and let that single verse from Psalm 33 sink in. The earth is full of God's unfailing love. This world—this broken, dis-

eased, corrupted, inequitable, uncertain, catastrophe-prone world—
is loved by God. The way he loves it is by loving and promoting
righteousness and justice. God knows it is not too late for the world.
Berlin may smolder—until it is rebuilt. A girl in India may be held
as a sexual slave—until someone rescues her. Malaria may kill
children—until generous people purchase mosquito netting for a
whole nation in sub-Saharan Africa. A socially awkward teenager
may be bullied at school—until parents and school administrators
take a stand against it. A drug addict may get released from jail one
more time, vulnerable to the same pattern of addiction and crime—
until he finds an effective recovery program that includes a loving
community.

Injustice corrodes our humanity wherever we experience it. This
is not the way things were supposed to be. Adam and Eve weren't
supposed to disobey God. Cain wasn't supposed to kill his brother
Abel. One out of seven people in the world should not go to bed hungry tonight because of problems of politics and distribution. We have
to be indignant about injustice in order to be champions of justice.

Across history human beings have shown just how many ways
the crooked and darkened soul can mess things up. And so the call
of God comes. He has shown us what is good and what he requires.
Do justice, love mercy, walk humbly. Make things right—whenever
you can, wherever you can.

If we have the potential to make things right (in any measure),
one would think that we would clamor for the opportunity. But
rightness and justice cut against human nature because they come
with a cost. Making things right is always right but never easy.

The law of the jungle seems to be the natural way of the world.
Eat or be eaten. Kill or be killed. Might makes right. Grab before
someone else takes. Hoard because you don't know if your supply
will run low. Follow the inverted golden rule (he who has the gold,
rules).

It is telling that we have so many ways of expressing this fatalistic
view of life. Frighteningly, this fatalistic view neither remembers nor
respects righteousness. Shame on us when we acquiesce to it in the
name of being "realists."

Great Objects

On a spring day in 1786 three men were walking the grounds of a beautiful English estate, talking about troubles and injustices in their country. They were all politicians—the prime minister, William Pitt; the future prime minister, William Grenville; and a member of Parliament, William Wilberforce. They were each just twenty-seven years old.[1]

As they paused in their conversation at the base of a large old oak tree, Wilberforce came to a fateful decision he had been weighing for weeks. He resolved to put on the table of Parliament the abolition of the slave trade—a momentous decision which would have world-changing ramifications, but which at that time was a life-risking move.

This just cause was looking for a champion in a position of influence. Abolitionists already had begun to denounce the practice of stealing men, women, and children from the African continent to work the British-owned sugarcane fields of the Caribbean. However, there was formidable economic and political resistance to the idea of stopping the lucrative slave trade. The cause was looking for a voice with real conscience. Though a small man, often ill, William Wilberforce was the perfect person to put the spotlight on a grave evil, to say, "This is not right. This must be set right." His five-foot frame was not impressive, but his public speech was, causing a surprised James Boswell to call Wilberforce a "shrimp" who when he spoke took on the stature of a "whale."

The young MP would not have taken up the cause were it not for a spiritual awakening. For the previous few years, Wilberforce had gone on a serious spiritual quest, reading Scripture, studying classic Christian writings, and talking to trusted friends. Among them was John Newton, the elderly pastor and former slave ship captain who had dramatically converted from a life of slave trading to a life devoted to being a humble servant of God. The spirit of Newton is summed up in the classic hymn he wrote: "Amazing Grace." The

---

1. For a full telling of the story, see Eric Metaxas, *Amazing Grace: William Wilberforce and the Heroic Campaign to End Slavery* (San Francisco: Harper One, 2007).

world has Newton to thank for convincing Wilberforce to stay in politics after his spiritual conversion.

On the day that Wilberforce rose to speak in Parliament and with precision, logic, and great detail first put forward the matter of abolishing the slave trade, he had no idea that it would take twenty long years of debate and toil and heartbreak before the slave trade would be made illegal. It would be another twenty-six years before existing slaves were actually emancipated. It shocks us today to think that the English population could know what they did at the time and not demand change. Abolitionists had obtained drawings of slave ships which showed the cruel techniques of confining hundreds of slaves under deck, lined up like wooden logs, and chained together. People were hearing about the misery and the stench, the disease which ravaged the Africans during their weeks-long passage across the Atlantic. They heard about one captain who threw living slaves overboard in order to collect insurance money.

But it was a horrifically coarse culture at the time. Wilberforce had two great goals in his life. He made this entry in his journal in 1787: "God Almighty has set before me two great objects, the suppression of the Slave Trade and the Reformation of Manners [moral values]." Wilberforce not only opposed slavery; he also worked to improve the culture of a people who relished the entertainment of public hangings, of public dissection of dead criminals, and of bloody animal spectacles including the practice of bull-baiting (bulls being torn apart by thick-jowled dogs in public squares). Corruption and immorality were widespread—a fourth of the women of London worked as prostitutes. The aristocratic class protected their privileges with no thought of equity or justice. And no one had ever thought that social justice might be the proper business of a legislative body.

What Wilberforce accomplished went far beyond the abolition of the slave trade—as amazing as that was. He introduced the seminal idea that social consciousness was part of the proper business of legislative bodies and political powers. The ideal jumped across the Atlantic to the newly formed United States of America. Decades later Abraham Lincoln would acknowledge the powerful influence of the small-statured MP of England, William Wilberforce.

Injustice Today

Many people today believe that William Wilberforce and Abraham Lincoln solved the problem of slavery. However, more human beings live in bondage today than at any other time of history. This includes people in impoverished parts of the world who have to pledge themselves against a loan that they will never be able to pay off. They labor, and their children labor, as the debt is passed to the next generation. It includes women and children held as slaves in sex industries, robbed of all dignity, deprived of all freedom. It includes forced labor where people are simply held against their will. Human beings are no longer sold as chattel on auction blocks, but it is still slavery when people are overpowered, dominated, and exploited.

As in Wilberforce's day there is a rising conscience, a righteous voice, against the wicked injustice of human trafficking. But as in Wilberforce's day, governments are not inclined to take action, and so justice takes place when courageous people infiltrate and confront brothels, or farms worked by slaves, or factories where bonded laborers are used like animals. Doing justice sometimes happens one rescue at a time.

We can get frozen by the question, What can we do in the face of overwhelming global injustice? Marry that to a belief that God is only interested in saving souls, not bodies, and we likely will do nothing. And join that to the ever-present self-interest in our hearts, and we will turn our backs on the widow, the fatherless, the foreigner, and the poor — four archetypes of human need mentioned numerous times in the Old Testament. Or we can recall Jesus' revolutionary words as he describes the time when the Son of Man returns to earth:

> "Then the King will say to those on his right, 'Come, you who are blessed by my Father; take your inheritance, the kingdom prepared for you since the creation of the world. For I was hungry and you gave me something to eat, I was thirsty and you gave me something to drink, I was a stranger and you invited me in, I needed clothes and you clothed me, I was sick and you looked after me, I was in prison and you came to visit me.'
>
> "Then the righteous will answer him, 'Lord, when did we see

you hungry and feed you, or thirsty and give you something to drink? When did we see you a stranger and invite you in, or needing clothes and clothe you? When did we see you sick or in prison and go to visit you?'

"The King will reply, 'Truly I tell you, whatever you did for one of the least of these brothers and sisters of mine, you did for me.'"

—*Matthew 25:34–40*

All of us can apply the simple practicality in this passage. The servants of the king did two things: they *saw*, and they *acted*. In whatever sphere of influence any of us occupy, we can and must do the same thing. To see and to act. Opening our eyes means being willing to look at the difficult scenes around us, the family tragedies, the tangled social policies, the abusive relationships and abuse of power, the pain of the oppressed, the loneliness of the dispossessed. Seeing includes serious research and moral curiosity. And then we choose how to act—for the person within a mile of where we live, and on behalf of people who live thousands of miles away.

The commitment to make things right is a fundamental form of spiritual influence. We need to take any small part of the world where we can make a difference, set aside any hesitation, and act. If we do not feel up to the task, that is understandable, because the only real power we have is what God gives. God makes things right with us and then commands us to act on what is right in his eyes. Do justice, love mercy, walk humbly. We don't act merely from a guilty conscience (which always results in a weak and temporary impact), but because we are influenced by God's own relentless hope for the world. "The LORD loves righteousness and justice; the earth is full of his unfailing love" (Ps. 33:5).

Chapter 9

SPEAK INTO CRISES

> In all this you greatly rejoice, though now for a little while you may have had to suffer grief in all kinds of trials. These have come so that the proven genuineness of your faith—of greater worth than gold, which perishes even though refined by fire—may result in praise, glory and honor when Jesus Christ is revealed.
>
> —*1 Peter 1:6–7*

Crisis opens us like an earthquake cracking the crust of the earth. A crisis is a time to decide, a turning point. Crisis moments require spiritual responsiveness and open a whole new opportunity for sustained spiritual influence. Crisis is where we learn about our base instincts, because people's hearts are torn open, what is inside comes out, and new truths and values may enter in.

Of all the formative influences in people's spiritual lives, the experience that is the most influential is crisis. People never forget a heartrending, danger-ridden passage—a true crisis—and what they learned about faith during and after that time. The most deforming experiences in life often turn out to be the most formative.

The Ministry of Presence

Time and again in the Scriptures, what God says in times of crisis is: I am here. I will not abandon you. You are not alone.

The LORD replied, "My Presence will go with you, and I will give you rest."   —*Exodus 33:14*

The LORD is close to the brokenhearted and saves those who are crushed in spirit.   —*Psalm 34:18*

God is our refuge and strength, an ever-present help in trouble.
                                                                                            —*Psalm 46:1*

God has said, "Never will I leave you; never will I forsake you." So we say with confidence, "The Lord is my helper; I will not be afraid. What can mere mortals do to me?"   —*Hebrews 13:5–6*

Helping people at a time of crisis is founded on the ministry of presence—of being there, in full awareness, responsiveness, and empathy. For any leader who is an activist at heart, the ministry of presence can seem like too little. Almost an insult. How can just "being there" be meaningful and effective? What does it accomplish? An emergency room physician can revive someone whose heart has stopped beating, a fireman can extinguish deathly flames, a policeman can put a criminal behind bars. These kinds of assistance in the face of crisis seem valuable to us. Leaders like to fix things.

But when crisis first breaks, it is not about fixing. Spiritual life and influence can make a life-changing difference when the earthquake of crisis hits, but it often comes in the form of the ministry of presence.

When the Hebrew people were wandering in the desert wilderness for years—anxious about water, food, enemies, disease—God offered the most important thing: his presence. He made his presence tangible in the form of the tent called the tabernacle. "Then have them make a sanctuary for me, and I will dwell among them" (Exod. 25:8). The tabernacle reminds his people that God chooses to live in and among them. He calls home whatever we call home—even if it is no home. Our lives are always on the move as we walk and search and battle and plod. Our one hope is that the God of heaven above is with us. Look at that tent over there. That was God's idea, not ours.

God keeps pitching tents, staying with people. Summing up the ministry and mission of Jesus, John said: "The Word became flesh and made his dwelling among us" (John 1:14). The word *dwell* in this verse means to pitch a tent, an obvious allusion back to the wilderness wanderings. Here is the same God doing the same thing. He lives among us. His presence matters. And so does the presence of people exercising spiritual influence.

We must put out of our minds any feeling that just "being there" is pitifully inadequate. If you've ever been in a crisis, you understand how important the presence of others is. In spiritual leadership we are called all the time into situations we cannot fix. No one can reverse the stillbirth; no one can compel a serial adulterer to love his spouse; no one can undo a bankruptcy. What we can do is help people take next steps, or enlist the help of others. But the first thing in response to crisis must be this: go there, be there, care. Leaders are often called to help people out of their own helplessness.

> I lift up my eyes to the mountains—
>   where does my help come from?
> My help comes from the LORD,
>   the Maker of heaven and earth.
>
> *—Psalm 121:1–2*

The measurement of the ministry of presence consists in thousands of people in thousands of situations who have said to a leader: Thank you for coming. Thank you for being here. And they will remember that for years to come.

When we perceive the need and respond by closing the gap, our presence may be what carries people in crisis across the chasm. That is the call of spiritual leadership in that moment, at that time. People appreciate the simple ministry of presence because aloneness and isolation are among the most painful spiritual experiences.

Call It What It Is

Have you ever been to a funeral where people go through verbal gymnastics in order to refer to a death as anything other than death? The deceased "has gone home to be with the Lord," or "has gone to meet her maker," or "has departed this ugly world," or "has gone to a better place." At least those are more delicate than some of the other euphemisms, which one will not generally hear in eulogies: kicked the bucket, belly up, six feet under, bought the farm, pushing up the daisies, at room temperature, gone to the big ranch in the sky, croaked.

We should avoid euphemisms that are mild expressions substituted for unpleasant realities. Likewise, we should avoid circumlocution, which is the use of many words with the intent of being vague or evasive. "Your mother was just too good for this imperfect world."

In crisis people don't want word games. They want honesty. They need to come to terms with harsh realities so that they are driven to their true resources in God. For example, after a suicide we would tend to avoid using the word *suicide*. Here is where we walk a tightrope: For the parents of a teen who committed suicide, the very idea is beyond horror, but God has made the human psyche capable of protecting itself temporarily through psychic numbing or even denial. To make it through the storm, however, the parents are going to have to name the thing. And the way they will be able to is when supportive people around them hold them up and protect them from the guilt, shame, and anger so that the dreaded reality of the situation can be called what it is.

If a leader needs to fire an employee, he must do so with honesty in order to protect his own integrity, the integrity of the organization, and even the integrity of the poor person who is cut. Call it what it is. If it is downsizing, call it downsizing. If it is failure, name what has gone wrong. If it is reorganization, call it that.

As Christians, we sometimes think that shading the truth is an act of mercy. We must remember that Jesus Christ came and he was "full of grace and truth." It is not grace instead of truth, but grace with truth.

When we speak honestly in a crisis, we help people prepare for the next crisis. We help people (and ourselves) accept reality. We get our heads out of the clouds and put our feet squarely on the ground. We are naming and recognizing the abnormal.

Speaking with Care

Christian character requires us to use discretion in the words we use (Prov. 18:13). Discretion is the quality of taking care so as not to cause offense unnecessarily. Leaders who use discretion are like surgeons who go into an operation with that uppermost value of the ancient Code of Hippocrates: "First: do no harm."

Some leaders make their mark in the world by speaking with provocative, blustering language. They make a big noise, and they keep doing it because it always turns heads. They may take their boisterous ways into crises. They may even get on the evening news. The indiscreet leader may even want to offend. He is always looking for effect. Either that, or he is too lazy to guard his words or too unskilled in using words in the first place. Some people just should not open their mouths.

Speaking into crisis is an extraordinary privilege and a great responsibility. When people's hearts are torn open, there is a window of opportunity for the right words to plant deep truths because— in that fleeting moment when people are wounded by crisis—they are looking for something or someone beyond. Something ultimate. Something that saves. But that window closes very quickly. The funeral is over, and twenty-four hours later everybody is back to work. The World Trade Center collapses and millions of people are aghast, church attendance jumps up for two weeks, maybe three or four. But then life goes on. Our attention span is very short.

But subconsciously people will have a spiritual memory of times of personal, family, or national crisis. These moments are not really forgotten. When people remember that crisis, and also recall one wise, truthful, and grace-filled thing a leader said in the middle of it, then they will know they can get through the next crisis.

When a Hurricane Hits

Everybody knew it was coming. Satellites took hour-by-hour snapshots of the spiral monster in the Gulf of Mexico. It fed on the energy of warm currents, it grew, it intensified. It drove toward the coast. The best scientific minds tried to estimate the surge of water coming and the winds of Hurricane Katrina—and where she would make landfall. When the levees broke, the city broke.

What happened next was an astonishing series of leadership miscalculations. The municipal government of New Orleans was unprepared. The state government of Louisiana assumed too much of the local government. The federal government assumed it had time after the disaster hit to figure out what to do. There were problems of miscommunication. Someone came up with a ridiculous plan to have refugees head to the football stadium for sanctuary, which resulted in twenty-five thousand people being left there for days without food, water, or medical assistance. And then the dark side of human nature took advantage of the void with looting, shootings, and random mayhem. Government leaders used the microphone for rhetoric, and then blaming.

All the while this natural disaster busted the fragile structures of government, a remarkable movement of individual saviors began. We did not see it on the television cameras right away, but hundreds of churches in the region sprang into action. Like the jazz music that is the soul of New Orleans, churches and small organizations improvised, doing what they could as circumstances changed with every passing hour. And it was remarkable how much they could do. Long before temporary housing was set up by the government, Christian groups were sheltering refugees. Food was distributed—homemade in church basement kitchens.

Pastor Dino Rizzo of Healing Place Church in Baton Rouge had already been working for days mobilizing the members of his congregation for emergency care. They ordered enough food for seven to eight thousand people, got on the phone and sent out emails getting hundreds of volunteers ready, and encouraged other congregations to get ready to work. A small network of like-minded and like-hearted people were ready—larger than one church, smaller than a government agency. More than a million evacuees were fleeing the city in advance of the high winds, ten inches of rain, and fifteen feet of water. Cooking for Christ, the church's food ministry, produced hundreds of meals for people who stopped in the church's parking lot. Volunteers walked down the gridlocked freeway passing out meals to stranded motorists.

Within three days, Rizzo and others had gotten more than four hundred churches mobilized. His perspective: it's amazing what can happen when no one gets the credit. The tools were basic: food, clothing, chain saws, medical equipment, generators. The motive was simple: Christ-followers cannot be idle in the face of suffering. The response was fast.

Being Ready

Responding to crisis is one of the greatest opportunities for authentic and effective spiritual leadership. Many people are ready to give up on finding spiritual truth and integrity. Long ago they tuned out religious rhetoric, and they wonder whether people with secular values are more concerned about real life than those with spiritual values. But here is the opportunity: When believers see themselves as first responders to crisis, and allocate their resources and energies in that direction, they will be used by God in decisive ways. And the response must be genuine, not because it looks good for PR, or with the idea that their acts of mercy are a method to prove the gospel.

There is a better way, a simpler way. Be ready—for whatever may happen. Don't view crises as interruptions of the work; they are the work. Mobilize people. Encourage them to act with compassion.

Crises focus our attention and force us to move to the margin everything that is marginal in life. If leaders see crises as interruptions to the work they are trying to get done, then they miss the most important work that can be done. Whether the setting is a church, a business, a school, or a nonprofit organization, an unexpected crisis is an opportunity to minister to the spirit of those who belong to that community. If leaders cultivate a culture of service and generosity, then when the crisis comes, people are ready to move.

Most important, in our better moments of spiritual influence, we are helping each other in the hard training for what lies ahead in life. If we start to get ready to deal with crisis when the crisis hits, we're too late.

In part 1 we looked at getting grounded for spiritual leadership. We must understand the call, learn to follow, engage with God, and build integrity. In part 2 we discussed taking initiative—some of the action steps of spiritual influence. That includes exploring new horizons, streaming ideas, seizing opportunities, making things right, and speaking into crises.

But when we look at leadership as a spiritual dynamic, which means being instruments for God's influence in the lives of people and recognizing their spiritual nature, there is another opportunity and necessity for us: going deep. This is the subject we will come to now in part 3. Influence means going deep, as deep as we can possibly go, into human nature and into the dynamic relationship of people and their creator. That is where the flowing-in happens. God's Spirit flows into us qualities like wisdom, truth, and power, and then we have something substantial to offer others.

When we go deep we find that we are dealing with three enormously powerful engines: power, authority, and truth. What we find in the history of humanity is that these three can be at the heart of good, constructive leadership, or they can be seductive, twisted, and ruinous.

When we go deep, we don't know what we will encounter.

Part 3

GOING
DEEP

Chapter 10

DEVELOP DISCERNMENT

Discernment is not a matter of simply telling the difference between right and wrong; rather it is telling the difference between right and almost right.

—Charles Spurgeon

Detectives or people trained in the art of espionage see things that other people do not. You may be able to recall a scene in a book, film, or TV drama where some astute observer looks around a room and evaluates every person, picking up clues as to who is a friend, who is a threat, or what has happened in that room. That person simply sees subtleties that ordinary people do not: the way a person glances away, the posture someone takes in the corner of the room, the manner of interactions between people. These finely tuned powers of observation are astonishing, and someone in the story is awed that the detective or spy can perceive mere hints of intent and motive. Often in such stories the protagonist is training the apprentice in the fine art of observation—of seeing reality at a deeper level.

Discernment is not only helpful to detectives; it is also a critically important spiritual ability and gift. Being an astute observer, capable of looking at a situation and seeing below the surface, is indispensable in the task of spiritual leadership. The Scriptures speak of gifts of discernment, knowledge, and wisdom. It is a seeing that goes deeper — down to people's strengths and weaknesses, values and motivations.

Put it another way: leaders with no discernment can do tremendous damage in a short amount of time. When we make decisions without discerning the way things really are, those decisions can be a waste of time or, worse, lead people down dangerous paths. For instance:

- A group of midlevel leaders is subjected to a lofty but unrealistic vision of their superior leader. Most of them have heard the rhetoric before because this leader's pattern is to raise the stakes by using the most outrageous aspirations, but actually the leader has a track record of halfway successes. A few of the midlevel leaders see what is going on under the surface. They discern the desperation and insecurity in the rhetoric. The "vision" is paraded out as an impossible goal that only God can accomplish, but it really is not the direction the Spirit of God wants to take the organization. It is just personal ambition run amok. But no one dares speak up, and discernment lingers in the minds of a few observers and is never honestly applied.
- A church leader receives from a member of the congregation waves of flattery, even fawning. It feels good. It feels like salve applied to the wounds of more troubling relationships. But the leader does not see that the desire of the flatterer is to attach himself or herself like a leech onto the leader. Two egos get stroked — one by dependency, the other by rescuing. At some point, however, flattery turns to resentment because of the vacuousness of the relationship, and it ends up a terrible mess. The mistake could have been avoided — if the leader had had the discernment to perceive the reasons for the flattery in the first place.
- Someone deeply struggling because of a conflict approaches a leader to lay out a long and complicated story of injury. The leader listens for most of an hour, shaking her head, clicking her tongue, and pouring out empathy. The hurt person

rewards her with tearful gratitude. The leader acts on what she has learned, confronting a fellow leader who is the offending party. But weeks later she hears the other side of the story and now is kicking herself for blanket assumptions she made. It is not the first time this has happened. She wonders why she so often hears one side of a story and takes it all at face value when she has seen so many times that there are always two sides to every story. She realizes she was lazy and afraid to dig out the truth. She did the easy thing—react—when she could have done the responsible thing, discern.

One of the greatest responsibilities leaders have is to guide people into clearer understandings of reality. To see things the way they really are. To see faults and failures for what they are, and hopes and horizons that are realistic as well. Leaders can only do that to the degree that they themselves distinguish true and false versions of reality. This is the skill and gift of discernment: clear perception and penetrating insight leading to good judgment.

How much we all need incisive leadership today! *Incisive* is a great word, the root of which means "cutting" or "penetrating" (from Latin *incidere*: to cut into). It is exactly the idea of the New Testament word for discernment (Greek *diakrina*), which means separation or distinction. The discerning leader approaches challenges and opportunities with a mental and spiritual scalpel. To be discriminating without being discriminatory. To judge without being judgmental. To separate without severing.

Discernment is delicate work.

The discerning leader looks at a situation, not rushing to judgment but being bold enough to eventually make a judgment by separating reality from perception. Good leaders know that perceptions matter and have to be dealt with, but what really matters is the truth—reality. We can be tempted to think of spiritual life as quite subjective, especially given the axiom today that there are many "truths" (even apparently contradictory "truths") in a given situation. But a surgeon in the operating room has to sever exactly the right tissue, a pilot navigating a valley needs to discern exactly the terrain of that valley, and an engineer needs to decide on exactly the right material to build a stable skyscraper. If incisive discernment is necessary in physical matters, how much more so in spiritual matters. No one benefits when we speak into a world that does not exist.

While errors will happen, they should never be because we were too quick or too lazy to do the scanning, probing, testing, balancing, consulting, praying work of discernment.

A True Spiritual Gift

Discernment is sometimes a quick and instinctive judgment, other times a complex, refined, and difficult process. Discernment is a true spiritual gift. A leader must try to approach situations with no bias or prejudice, even though the leader's identity and ego are frequently tangled in many leadership challenges. Discernment means looking deeply into important matters, as deep as the human spirit itself. Hebrews 4:12 describes the sharp edge of discernment: "The word of God is alive and active. Sharper than any double-edged sword, it penetrates even to dividing soul and spirit, joints and marrow; it judges the thoughts and attitudes of the heart."

Now when people exercise judgment over our attitudes, thoughts, or behaviors, we often recoil—a natural enough reaction. Then we wonder whether the person sizing us up had the right to confront us. We end up discerning the discerner. In some situations the confrontation is proper because it is the designated job of the confronter (in the case of a supervisor, for instance). Or the Spirit of God has truly prompted the confrontation. Other times, critics aren't being judicious, just judgmental.

So what do we do when someone confronts us, and we know immediately that the person is right? Our ability to receive the confrontation will depend on whether we view it as a matter of the truth of God, or just an exchange between two people. This is why discernment is a distinctly spiritual movement. If we are going to be evaluated, corrected, or encouraged—we want God to be the influencer, not just another human being. The Word of God is sharper than a sword—not us.

The list of spiritual gifts in 1 Corinthians 12 includes "distinguishing between spirits" (v. 10), which means that Christian leaders need to discern the distinctions between good and evil intent. Making the same point, 1 John 4:1 instructs us to "test the spirits to see whether they are from God, because many false prophets have gone out into the world." Hebrews 5:14 speaks of mature believers "who by constant use have trained themselves to distinguish good from evil." These passages signal that we will be exposed to many things worse than "bad influences." Some of the most powerful leaders in the history of the world have been evil and counterfeit. Throngs of people have followed, marching to a drumbeat that has almost hypnotic effects. We all know that evil influencers, in the name of God or religion, have inspired theft and corruption, murder and suicide. Such stories may seem far away. But the next cult leader is as close to us as the hidden lie. Evil needs nothing more than ordinary people who turn off discernment because of the allure of lavish promises.

Paul promises that the Spirit of God will give us the mind of Christ, and then we will be capable of authentic spiritual discernment. "The person without the Spirit does not accept the things that come from the Spirit of God but considers them foolishness, and cannot understand them because they are discerned only through the Spirit. The person with the Spirit makes judgments about all things, but such a person is not subject to merely human judgments, for 'Who has known the mind of the Lord so as to instruct him?' But we have the mind of Christ" (1 Cor. 2:14–16). This is a great description of spiritual influence. As the Spirit "flows in," our hearts and minds are completely reshaped such that we gain an ability to see reality more accurately and at a deeper level. We see things that the natural mind just does not perceive. This "in-fluence" is profound, deep, and enduring. And it becomes the basis of our influence on others.

One of the most significant decisions any of us make, one where discernment can spell the difference between flourishing and ruin, is whether we will entrust ourselves to be influenced by someone else—a question we'll face in many different settings.

- Should I trust that my boss knows what she is doing?
- What book will give me an authoritative answer to my question?

- Why do I have mixed feelings when I listen to that preacher?
- Should I vote for candidate A or candidate B?
- Should I take this job even though I am getting mixed signals on whether they want me?
- Is the theology of that blogger trustworthy?
- This group is telling me there is a systemic problem in our organization — are they right, or are they malcontents who have found each other?

Discernment is a kind of penetrating vision that helps us see through the dust and fog of life, to see things the way they really are, and to make conscious choices about the people we want to influence us. Discernment is perception, insight, and correct judgment about the people wanting to influence us. We have to be discerning, and then we must recognize that other people will be doing the same thing with us: sizing us up, looking for consistency, probing for motive.

So let's say you have to decide whether to let someone advise you and consult with you about what you do. What does discernment look like in a situation where another person's opinion could have a major impact on how you do things? With no discernment, you will make that decision based on factors like these: Is this person popular with other people? Will I be viewed by others as more credible if I listen to this person? Will this consultation make my life easier? Will the advice of this person free me from making the tough decisions I am facing? Exercising discernment in a decision like this, however, would lead us to look deeper before trusting an outside advisor or consultant, to ask questions like, What are the values of this person, and are they compatible with mine? Has this person had a beneficial impact on others in a similar situation? Do I understand the motives of this person? Does this person care enough to work hard to understand my situation?

Discernment Today

Today people of influence are able to get away with actions that have little integrity and no discernment because of the increasing distance between them and the people they lead. In an age of virtual platforms where there is little personal accountability, influencers are often two-dimensional figures whose deep values and motives are obscured. The TV screen flattens; the internet offers a screen behind which the Wizard of Oz pushes the buttons and pulls the levers. The conference spotlight illuminates a body, but not a life. The sheer size of some organizations shields leaders from real evaluation by their constituencies.

And then there are the driving motivations of our competitive culture. Applause comes when somone gets results, whether they are founded on discernment or not. We are satisfied with image, when we should insist on transformation. Microphones add a false resonance to the voices of influencers whose highest skill is merely stepping onto the stage.

But there is hope. All the tools and techniques of the world today, though they can be used to obfuscate, obscure, detract, shield, deceive, and manipulate, are also a powerful means of a ministry of discernment to the masses. Today our tools of communication give us access to thousands of perspectives—we just need to use discernment to find them.

And there is one other significant issue today: judgmentalism.

This is a make-or-break issue for many, particularly young adults. Many perceive Christian faith to be an exercise in bias, partisanship, and intolerance. This is tragic when it is true, and tragic when it is mere perception. Scripture leaves us with two challenging principles: leaders must exercise judgment (i.e., discernment), but we must not be judgmental. But what is the dividing line between the two?

It is right there in the Sermon on the Mount: "Do not judge, or you too will be judged. For in the same way you judge others, you will be judged, and with the measure you use, it will be measured to you" (Matt. 7:1–2). And then comes Jesus' famous confrontation: How can you dare point out a speck in another's eye, when you've got a whole board protruding from yours?

On the other hand, believers are encouraged to make judgments—a far better path, for instance, than taking conflicts to the civil courts: "Do you not know that the Lord's people will judge the world? And if you are to judge the world, are you not competent to judge trivial cases? Do you not know that we will judge angels? How much more the things of this life!" (1 Cor. 6:2–3).

So here is the fine line we must walk: judging, but not being judgmental. Romans 14 helps us understand the difference. Judgment has crossed the line when it condemns people for matters that are not transgressions (the issue in this passage being matters of devotion), and it has gone too far when it supplants God's role as final arbiter.

> You, then, why do you judge your brother or sister? Or why do you treat them with contempt? For we will all stand before God's judgment seat. It is written:
>
> > " 'As surely as I live,' says the Lord,
> > 'every knee will bow before me;
> >   every tongue will acknowledge God.' "
>
> So then, each of us will give an account of ourselves to God.
> Therefore let us stop passing judgment on one another.
> —*Romans 14:10–13*

So, discernment, but not judgmentalism.

Are there things we can do to deepen the skill of discernment? In a deeply personal letter written from prison, the apostle Paul showed how he longed for his friends to grow in discernment. "And this is my prayer: that your love may abound more and more in knowledge and depth of insight, so that you may be able to discern what is best and may be pure and blameless for the day of Christ" (Phil. 1:9–10).

Here are some clues about how we can deepen the skill of discernment, which does not come to us out of thin air. We need to accumulate an abundance of knowledge, to be perpetual learners about life and leadership. Knowledge will not automatically make us discerning, but it is impossible to have discernment if our knowledge base is narrow.

"Depth of insight" is also an accumulating resource. If we are continually engaged in conversation with other leaders, listening for the insights they have accumulated through experience, we will train our vision. Some people are satisfied with a surface understanding of life; the people who do the work to go deep and accumulate refined insights are as good as gold.

And our skills in discernment will grow over time if we value — and pursue — that God-given treasure Scripture speaks so frequently about: wisdom.

Chapter 11

PURSUE WISDOM

Not until we have become humble and teachable, standing in awe of God's holiness and sovereignty, acknowledging our own littleness, distrusting our own thoughts, and willing to have our minds turned upside down, can divine wisdom become ours.

—*J. I. Packer*

You just finished your work for the day, which included a difficult meeting about a thorny problem. The discussion had gone around in circles. People were frustrated. But when it came time for you to talk, you felt as though God helped you to be smarter than yourself. As you expressed yourself, people were paying close attention, some nodding their heads. You saw the problem from a different angle, and you offered a solution that had the ring of truth to it. At the end, someone said to you, "Where did you get that kind of wisdom?" You go home thinking to yourself, "Now *that* was a good day."

The windswept spot was high above the plain and separate from the recently established City of David, seven miles distant. Gibeon was a place of worship in the early days of Israel's kings, and the Tent of Meeting, the traveling symbol of the traveling God originally built by Moses hundreds of years earlier, was pitched there. Solomon had gone to Gibeon to offer sacrifices. A substantial kingdom was finally taking shape and was ready to be turned over to the next generation after David. Representatives of all the tribes, all the clans, the army, and the judges had assembled. It was a pivotal moment in history.

In the middle of the night God appeared to Solomon at Gibeon, saying: "Ask for whatever you want me to give you" (1 Kings 3:5; 2 Chron. 1:7).

This offer must have seemed too good to be true. "Whatever?"

What might a brand-new leader want in order to make the responsibility laid on his shoulders doable? A large treasury? The largest army in the world? Submission by all the surrounding kings?

But Solomon wanted something different: "Give me wisdom and knowledge, that I may lead this people, for who is able to govern this great people of yours?" (2 Chron. 1:10). We hear in these words a degree of trepidation and pleading. Solomon knew the history of Israel, knew the impossibility of leading hundreds of thousands of people not just as a stable and prosperous country, but as a people of God. Leadership is difficult; spiritual leadership just makes things more complicated.

You know the rest of the story. God acknowledges that because Solomon chose not to ask for wealth, prestige, long life, or the death of his enemies, he would indeed receive wisdom and knowledge. And material prosperity came as well.

We often hear stories of heroes gaining wisdom from some wizened old master which equips them for the quest they have been called to. In Scripture, God replaces the master. Wisdom comes not from a mentor, but from the Creator. Solomon's wisdom is a divine gift; Joseph gets wisdom from God, not from Pharaoh. Daniel's story is the same. The newly converted Paul goes into a years-long period of preparation in Arabia in which he receives some kind of direct revelation.

Information can be put in a book. Wisdom is something bigger. It has a name. It has a voice. Proverbs 8 begins:

Does not wisdom call out?
  Does not understanding raise her voice?
At the highest point along the way,
  where the paths meet, she takes her stand;

beside the gate leading into the city,
     at the entrance, she cries aloud:
"To you, O people, I call out;
     I raise my voice to all mankind.
You who are simple, gain prudence;
     you who are foolish, set your hearts on it.
Listen, for I have trustworthy things to say;
     I open my lips to speak what is right.
My mouth speaks what is true,
     for my lips detest wickedness.
All the words of my mouth are just;
     none of them is crooked or perverse.
To the discerning all of them are right;
     they are upright to those who have found knowledge.
Choose my instruction instead of silver,
     knowledge rather than choice gold,
for wisdom is more precious than rubies,
     and nothing you desire can compare with her."

According to the book of Proverbs, wisdom is more than essential: it is a life-or-death matter. The alternative to wisdom is the life of the fool. And Proverbs is specific here on the nuances of foolishness. First, there is the naive person, someone who is easily led (fooled), is gullible, or simpleminded. This type of foolishness leads to irresponsibility and complacency, and a real risk of drifting into danger. The second kind of fool in Proverbs is the person who chooses not to listen, is disdainful of wisdom, disrespectful of authority, and impatient with advice. This attitude inevitably leads to folly. And the third kind of fool is the scoffer, someone who mocks what is good. This kind of foolishness goes beyond carelessness; it is to be an active destructive influence. Think about all the really bad leadership decisions you've witnessed, and chances are you'll find that many of them came out of simple foolishness. And the alarming thing is that society offers so few incentives to break patterns of foolishness. Wisdom has become optional.

Proverbs 18:4 says, "The fountain of wisdom is a rushing stream." Wisdom comes from a hidden, inexhaustible source; it is steady, it is abundant, it flows. Spiritual influence means the flowing in of wisdom's goodness and insight. Wisdom flows to us from God, and then it can and must flow from us to the people we are supposed to influence.

This influence comes to us from a hidden place. It is "God's wisdom, a mystery that has been hidden and that God destined for our glory before time began" (1 Cor. 2:7).

Wisdom Is at the Core of Spiritual Leadership

Some leaders are specially gifted in administration, others in teaching, others in strategic thinking, and so on. But one characteristic that should hold true of everyone who wishes to be a spiritual influence is growth in wisdom.

When the apostle Paul came to Greece he entered a culture supposedly based on sophisticated wisdom. Philosophy ("love of wisdom") was the basis of Greek society. But Paul reminded the believers in Corinth: "When I came to you, I did not come with eloquence or human wisdom as I proclaimed to you the testimony about God" (1 Cor. 2:1). Paul was a brilliant and educated man and could have used philosophy, but instead he took a different stance. "I resolved to know nothing while I was with you except Jesus Christ and him crucified" (1 Cor. 2:2). Grounded in history, centered in a great redemptive act, the fact of Jesus was the message.

In Jesus the primordial wisdom of God the Father is centered and flows to human beings by the Spirit of God. Father, Son, and Spirit bring to us a wisdom that is "secret" (i.e., mysterious) and that stands in the starkest contrast to "the wisdom of this age or of the rulers of this age, who are coming to nothing" (1 Cor. 2:6).

And so, Paul says, "This is what we speak, not in words taught us by human wisdom but in words taught by the Spirit, explaining spiritual realities with Spirit-taught words" (1 Cor. 2:13).

When God uses us as instruments of his influence in the lives of others, we realize how inadequate all the tools and techniques of generic leadership are—not necessarily invalid, just incomplete. We begin looking for the outcomes that God wants in every leadership challenge we face. We realize how much we don't know without the revelation of God. We appreciate the amazing wisdom of respected leaders who accomplish great things not just for next quarter's report, but for eternity.

The Wisdom from Heaven

In his epistle, James puts a spotlight on "the wisdom from above." He contrasts it with "earthly wisdom," which is so misguided that it leads to "envy and selfish ambition," "disorder," and "every evil practice" (James 3:16).

Then in one defining statement James identifies seven characteristics of this wisdom that comes from a source higher than ourselves. This could serve as a charter for everyone who is committed to basing their influence on wisdom. Here it is, brief but forceful: "But the wisdom that comes from heaven is first of all pure; then peace-loving, considerate, submissive, full of mercy and good fruit, impartial and sincere" (James 3:17). Like the book of Proverbs in the Old Testament, James offers precepts on a life shaped by divine wisdom. This is not theory and certainly not esoteric knowledge—it is practical in every way. And it is the substance of spiritual leadership.

So James 3:17 begins by saying the wisdom from above is "pure." The people we deem to be extraordinarily wise probably are people who are relatively free of mixed motives, are not driven by personal ambition, and have generous, stable attitudes. This is the meaning of purity, and it is what makes some people open conduits of God's wisdom. They don't mess things up with themselves. They look you in the eye and see you for who you are and not who they want you to be for them. (Application: leadership that is pure has a moral and ethical clarity.)

James 3:17 then says this spiritual wisdom is "peace-loving." Wise people are driven by a longing for and belief in reconciliation. They know what happens when someone finds peace with God. They make every effort to bring people together, to promote forgiveness and forbearance. Their wisdom steers them away from superficial peace because they know that the only thing worth seeking is the peace that "transcends all understanding" (Phil. 4:7). (Application: leadership that is peace-loving will bring people together rather than dividing and conquering.)

Next, the wisdom from above is "considerate." This is not mere politeness. Consideration for his people is a core characteristic of God in the Old Testament—he is the king who cares for his people at the same time that he rules them. (Application: leadership that is considerate is always humane—like God.)

This wisdom is also "submissive." This is not weakness, but the willingness to yield. It is the teachable attitude, the cooperative spirit, the opposite of obstinate self-confidence. (Application: leadership that is submissive is always improving because it is open to learning and changing.)

"Full of mercy and good fruit" is the next description in James 3:17. Wisdom is not passive. It propels people toward action, but not just any action. Wisdom gives us a vision to see real human need and to help those in need with practical acts of mercy. (Application: leadership that is full of mercy and good fruit is a gift to humanity.)

The wisdom that comes from God is "impartial." In a world where people get ahead through privilege, status, and connections, wisdom rejects the games and renounces favoritism. The unselfish character of wisdom makes it impartial. (Application: leadership that is impartial raises everyone above the seedy side of human manipulation.)

And finally, the "wisdom from above" is "sincere." Anhypokirtos—without hypocrisy. The word *hypocrite* means "actor." And today actors have more than one theater in which to put on their show. The television screen, the social networking website, and the jackets of hardcover books are ready-made stages. And what is played on those stages may be sincere or utterly false. (Application: leadership that is sincere is conspicuously honest, and thus able to engender trust and ultimately achieve higher purposes.)

So what then is wisdom? Both a special gift from God and a personal skill that is developed over time, wisdom is deep insight into the true nature of things, including their moral value, and the integrity to act on that insight. Wisdom is not different from knowledge, but is more than knowledge—like the difference between knowing about your spouse and *knowing* your spouse.

When leaders crave wisdom, they want their decisions to be morally good, not just measurably productive. They want to untangle problems others have given up on. They don't mind wading into seemingly unsolvable situations because they figure that someone has to start untangling the knots everyone is staring at.

Wise leaders naturally engender trust because they stream wisdom. They are not egotistical, because they are viscerally repulsed by arrogance. They are also brave enough to accept being confronted regarding their own moments of foolishness. Only fools never feel foolish.

One Wise Leader

Eugene Peterson is one of the most beloved Christian leaders today. His writings, including his translation of the Bible called *The Message*, have influenced millions — yet he avoids the limelight, rarely speaking at conferences, preferring the real-life, face-to-face interaction of ideas with a dozen people sitting in a room. He was the pastor of one church for twenty-nine years, trying faithfully to do what is central to shepherding: praying, teaching Scripture, visiting the sick. He experienced the highs and lows of ministry, offering his resignation when he could not reconcile the organizational demands of the church with his basic spiritual duties to the church and to his family, which led to a sounder approach to ministry, rather than resignation.

That church was Presbyterian, but he grew up in a small Pentecostal church in rural Montana, where he took in biblical truth along with a few spiritual aberrations. At the same time that he became a serious student of the Bible, he also had all his senses attuned to the robust world of nature in the great outdoors of Montana. Throughout his life, he has maintained an awe of the Creator because he chooses to be fully aware of the creation. The way he sees life and Genesis, childbirth and disease, work and rest all come from this wisdom made possible by a full attentiveness to all of life. Peterson insists that we be attuned to the real lives of the people we work with, be they bankers, farmers, scientists, students, or retirees. We minister to them not because they are customers, but because they are created.

He studies the Bible in Hebrew and Greek, content to teach a Sunday morning class of three people, and able to methodically translate the whole of the Old and New Testaments. He takes Scripture very seriously. Not as it bolsters preconceived theological positions, but as it creates a lively, fresh interaction with the reader. He sees the vividness of the truth. He is compelled by the life that the truth of God produces. And he insists on the way of Jesus. Way, truth, life. We know that this is how Jesus described himself (John 14:6). But Peterson insists that one cannot hold to the truth and the life without conducting ourselves in the way of Jesus.

Peterson's motives are conspicuously God-centered, which makes him a great role model. His definition of ministry is to be fully aware of the present—of what God is doing, of what people are doing, and of the potential connections. He is a lifelong learner, listening to what God is saying through whatever means (he chooses his mentors carefully—most of them having lived in previous centuries). And he is grounded in the Word of God. As a result his wisdom is sought by millions of people and will go on long after he has left this life.

Wisdom Today

Wisdom-based influence and leadership should be the norm. But in a time when we look for quick and splashy accomplishments, wisdom is not a headline issue. Wisdom is not a sexy word. Passion is. Vision is. But passion without wisdom can burn people up rather than getting them to burn on. And vision without wisdom can lead to arbitrary or unrealistic goals, driving down a road that ends off a cliff. In contrast, wisdom drives the boldest initiatives and strongest convictions. Wisdom is anything but tame.

We have this unfortunate metaphor for wisdom: the owl perched high in a tree. Unmoving. Mysterious. Aloof. That is a poor picture of wisdom. Better to think of the eagle, which, from a high altitude, is able to scan the details on the ground, ready to act in the blink of an eye. Wisdom is not just about getting answers, but about acting on them.

How Can We Make Sure Our Influence Is Rooted in Wisdom?

First, we must crave wisdom. God told Solomon he would give him anything, and instead of fortune or power, Solomon longed to have wisdom "to govern the people well." We need to ask ourselves if we truly value wisdom. Are we desperate for the spiritual skill to lead well? Do we admire wisdom wherever we find it? And when we meet really wise people, do we take the time to figure out how they got that way?

Second, we must ask for wisdom. James tells us, "If any of you lacks wisdom, you should ask God" (1:5). The smartest parents, teachers, managers, business owners, healthcare workers, pastors, and missionaries never assume they have reached a point in life where they are wise enough for every contingency. Wisdom cannot be the occasional bonus; it must be at the center of every leadership decision, small and large. No day should pass without asking God for wisdom. To look for wisdom only sometimes is to risk foolishness most times.

Seeking wisdom helps shape our prayer life as leaders. If we only pray for outcomes, we are short-circuiting the way God wants to help us achieve the best outcomes. We are told to pray for wisdom because God wants us to engage our minds and hearts in achieving those outcomes. And then we have been trained for the next opportunity. The classic prayer of spiritual leadership should be: "Lord, give me wisdom."

Third, we must pursue wisdom. When you're walking through a desert, all that matters is where the next source of water is. When we meditate on Scripture and study it deeply, we choose to come under the direct influence of wisdom. But when we read the Bible superficially, we will attain only a veneer of spirituality which allows us to "baptize" what we were planning on doing anyway. Investing time in the study of Scripture is one of the most loving things we can do for the people we influence. Reading the book of Proverbs and the book of James at least once a year would revolutionize our influence. We should also pursue the wisdom that other believers possess, which they are supposed to be giving away anyway. The Holy Spirit pours out spiritual insight on all kinds of believers, and he calls us to learn from each other. So we should pursue people who have wisdom — engage with them, pummel them with questions, find out how they think things through, beg them for prayer. And we should read the books of sages from the past. Sometimes dead people can be our best friends.

Pursuing wisdom takes time. It takes energy to get connected with other wise believers. But there is no substitute and there is no shortcut.

Chapter 12

RECEIVE POWER

> Nearly all men can stand adversity, but if you want to test a man's character, give him power.
> —*Abraham Lincoln*

Power, authority, truth. These are perilous words, distrusted by many. The nervousness comes not just from the skeptics who are well aware of the many contemporary and historic examples where people have been coercive in the name of religion. Well-intentioned Christian voices also warn about the inherent riskiness of power, authority, and truth. Some believe Christians should take a submissive and quietistic approach to influence because we are so easily corrupted when we get power in our hands.

As dangerous as power, authority, and truth may be, however, they are woven directly into the biblical narrative as influences that bear upon us, and ways that we influence others—with great care.

When we lead, we exercise power—and in spiritual influence this is a redirection of the power of God because any power we possess is puny by comparison, and dangerous as well.

When we lead, we assert authority—but the difference between transformational leadership and pathological leadership is whether we are helping people discover God's authority in their lives or we are just asserting our own authority.

When we lead, we declare truth—although in Christian faith "truth" is not a person's property or tool, but a faithful definition of reality that is to be shared, not imposed.

These three dynamics are at the nexus of divine and human influence. They are the topics of the next three chapters, and each of them determines the success or failure of influencers. Power, authority, and truth are the places where divine leadership and human leadership connect. We know intuitively that these are core issues, and that is backed up by what the Scriptures say.

Does the very notion of spiritual power, authority, and truth protect us, or expose us to greater risk? It can work either way. When a person believes his or her spiritual influence is founded on divine power, authority, and truth, they may be using a smokescreen to hide abuses. On the issue of power: as destructive as it is for leaders to assert *personal* power and charisma, it is many times more so when they convince throngs of people that they possess and control *divine* power. When it comes to authority, we can all think of how it has been abused to the extent that leaders have said—explicitly or implicitly—that when they speak, God is speaking. And then there is truth. Leaders abuse the truth when they control and manipulate people by convincing them that they have a secret knowledge, an esoteric understanding, that gives followers a special status and leads them into an exclusive community.

But when we believe that our very best obedience to God's call consists in letting God lead through us, then we remove ourselves from the equation, although this will be a lifelong struggle against our own tendency to keep making ourselves the issue. The divine/human nexus is what enabled a proud Pharisee, Saul of Tarsus, to be transformed into the apostle Paul, saying that his righteousness was so much rubbish (Phil. 3:8). As a Pharisee he was part of a tradition that claimed a privileged grasp of the truth of God, and with that, authority and power. But his conversion amounted to relinquishing his own truth, authority, and power in order to embrace Jesus as his truth, authority, and power. Laying down his own authority allowed him to see his limitations as his strength ("I will boast all the more gladly about my weaknesses, so that Christ's power may rest on me" [2 Cor. 12:9]). Because Christ's authority, power, and truth shone through Paul, Paul's influence was deep and enduring.

Do we not want that same lasting influence?

The Power of Power

J. R. R. Tolkien used a small object and a small person—a ring and a quaint creature known as a hobbit—as the focal points for his epic tale of the clash of kingdoms, *The Lord of the Rings*. The massive and complex story includes narrative arcs of war, corruption, and redemption. It is a story about power, its use and abuse. A set of magical rings was forged in ancient times, but the struggle to possess the rings and their special properties becomes a contest for power itself. So there is power, and the desire to possess it, which is a power in and of itself. Whoever comes into contact with "the one ring" becomes corrupted by it. The storyline includes a struggle between whole races to possess the ring, and naive characters who discover its captivating power by mistake. Some of the most powerful good characters resist the temptation to possess the ring. Gandalf the Wise says to the hobbit who wants the ring safeguarded: "Don't tempt me, Frodo. I dare not take it, not even to keep it safe. Understand, Frodo, I would use this ring from a desire to do good. But through me it would wield power too great and terrible to imagine." And when the hobbit offers the ring to the beautiful Galadriel, she rebuffs the offer, predicting: "You would have a queen—beautiful and terrible as the dawn, treacherous as the sea, stronger than the foundations of the earth. All shall love me and despair."

So goes the history of power. "Power corrupts; absolute power corrupts absolutely," as Lord Acton said in 1887.

Power is enormously complicated, because being an influence (or being an instrument for God's influence) does mean exercising power at some level. Unprincipled leadership is almost always all about power—gaining it, keeping it, using it. Spiritual leadership, on the other hand, means taking a powerless stance so as to receive and transmit the power of God.

The world has changed much in the past few decades, and that includes major power shifts. Power used to be centered almost exclusively in institutions and elite classes that controlled resources. It used to be that you needed to have an army to strike a military blow. Today one fanatic with high explosives in a hidden vest can blow himself up and terrorize a whole country. In the past, news, commentary, and information were controlled by newspapers and three or four television stations. Today there are hundreds of cable channels, and any blogger has the potential to be an influential voice to thousands of people.

Because of this we need to ask ourselves, Does the word *power* have positive or negative connotations for me? Why? Where have I seen power used to a positive end in God's kingdom work? Where have I seen power or position abused? Where have I seen the power of God displayed in a bold, unambiguous manner? In what ways am I confident about the power that comes with leadership, and what worries me about it?

Teaching about Power in the Ministry of Jesus

In the New Testament there are two closely related concepts: power and authority. Power is the ability to do something; authority is the right to do so. You may have at some time in the past worked for a boss who had the position or authority to exercise leadership, but had no ability (power) to do so (power without authority). Or you may have worked with someone who was able to exert force, but had no right to do so. Either scenario is an exercise in frustration and futility. Spiritual leadership is based on God-given ability (power) matched with God-defined purpose or mission (authority). What the world needs today is spiritual influence through which people flourish by God's power and authority.

It was a return visit to his hometown and the synagogue there. At the very start of his ministry Jesus had been to this synagogue. He read from Isaiah, announced that the kingdom of God had come, and was nearly thrown off a cliff. Now he was on a return visit, teaching in that same synagogue but now with the reputation that he had shown "miraculous power" all over Galilee. The people's response? "They were amazed. 'Where did this man get this wisdom and these miraculous powers?' they asked. 'Isn't this the carpenter's son? Isn't his mother's name Mary, and aren't his brothers James, Joseph, Simon and Judas? Aren't all his sisters with us? Where then did this man get all these things?'" (Matt. 13:54–56). But even with all that, "they took offense at him" (13:57).

The power of God in Jesus' deeds stunned people, as did the lightning-strike veracity of his spoken wisdom. People could still oppose him, but they could not ignore him.

Jesus repudiated arbitrary power. The greatest political, social, and military power in Jesus' day—the power of the Roman Empire— was the hammer Pontius Pilate applied to Jesus when he said, "Don't you realize I have power either to free you or to crucify you?" (John 19:10). Jesus' answer was not what Pilate expected: "You would have no power over me if it were not given to you from above" (v. 11).

Jesus conferred power on his twelve disciples, thereby setting the paradigm of spiritual leadership. Jesus "gave them power and author-ity to drive out all demons and to cure diseases" (Luke 9:1). This was not about showmanship, but a battle with evil. "I have given you authority ... to overcome all the power of the enemy" (Luke 10:19). Peter, James, and John must have been awed at the prospect, yet this was only a prelude to the world-changing power that would come to them. Before the ascension Jesus told them: "But you will receive power when the Holy Spirit comes on you; and you will be my witnesses in Jerusalem, and in all Judea and Samaria, and to the ends of the earth" (Acts 1:8). Jesus' purpose in giving power to his disciples is so that they will witness to others about him. This is a perfect example of a connecting point—a nexus—between divine and human influence. Acts of power by Jesus' followers are not ends in themselves, but pointers to the expansive power of God. We are providing a witness or testimony to the intent of God to restore human health and dignity. So when Peter healed a lame man in Acts 3, he took the opportunity for witness: "Fellow Israelites, why does this surprise you? Why do you stare at us as if by our own power or godliness we had made this man walk?" (Acts 3:12). The most pow-erful thing a person can do is to eschew personal power and let the power of God flow through in word and deed.

Teaching about Power in the Writings of Paul

Jesus ushered in the new era of the kingdom of God with astonishing demonstrations of the power of God; the apostle Paul explained a whole new ethic of life based on this new understanding of the power of God. His explanations of strength in weakness, wisdom that looks like foolishness, and power inherent in the gospel itself are nothing less than revolutionary. When Christian leaders base their influence on these truths about power, they are living in the nexus where their influence is dramatically more effective than if they acted as ordinary power brokers — and they will be protected from many of the corrupting effects of holding power.

The power of God gives us boldness. "I am not ashamed of the gospel, because it is the power of God that brings salvation to everyone who believes: first to the Jew, then to the Gentile" (Rom. 1:16). The gospel is the proclamation of God's redemptive work in Christ. It is a message, but not mere talk. This gospel is the power of God. It stuns people. Surprises them. Impacts them. Flows into them and through them, changing them forever. This proclamation that is power knocks down the proud, elevates the humble, empowers people who are disenfranchised. Paul probably would not have bothered calling himself merely a leader as we typically speak of leaders. He viewed himself as the herald of a great movement sweeping the earth that was entirely from God and about God. He witnessed a revolution unfolding that could never be attributed to human genius or power. It was too wide-ranging, too visionary, too penetrating for that.

In Paul's two letters to the church in Corinth, he speaks often about power, because Corinth was a center of Greek culture with all of its glories and its seediness. The "ways of the world" dominated Corinth, and so Paul took it as his mission to redefine power.

"The message of the cross is foolishness to those who are perishing, but to us who are being saved it is the power of God" (1 Cor. 1:18). Where is one to find the power of God? Paul was unequivocal: in the message, the gospel, which says that the sacrifice of Jesus has opened the way for people to be reconnected with their Creator. So Christ is "the power of God and the wisdom of God" (1 Cor. 1:24).

When we proclaim that, it is not mere talk. "The kingdom of God is not a matter of talk but of power" (1 Cor. 4:20). Paul reminds the Corinthian believers that when he brought the message to them, it was not with the techniques of eloquent speech (today we might say slick marketing, or cutting-edge communication). "My message and my preaching were not with wise and persuasive words, but with a demonstration of the Spirit's power" (1 Cor. 2:4).

Paul's second letter to the believers in Corinth has more personal passion, even angst. He pours out his heart about his wounds and weaknesses. And here again, it is the power of God in Christ that counts. Speaking of some undefined infirmity that he asked God to take away, Paul says he heard from God: "My grace is sufficient for you, for my power is made perfect in weakness." And so he concludes: "Therefore I will boast all the more gladly about my weaknesses, so that Christ's power may rest on me" (2 Cor. 12:9). Paul looked to the power of the crucified Christ as the key to unlocking his own weaknesses and many sufferings: "For to be sure, he was crucified in weakness, yet he lives by God's power. Likewise, we are weak in him, yet by God's power we will live with him in our dealing with you" (2 Cor. 13:4).

These are the truths that will make the difference between having effective spiritual influence and exercising leadership that merely moves people around. The power described in the Scriptures surpasses any secular notion of power. Frankly, this truth is hard to maintain in an era when investment bankers can make or break people's fortunes, when a B-2 bomber can incinerate a city, and when a media syndicate can pull the strings of a global leader. We see the exercise of blunt-edged power all the time, and those forms of power seem to gain energy from the supercharged atmosphere of today's world.

But at the same time God still displays his power in and through people. Billy Graham speaks powerful words in front of a million people in Seoul, Korea. Mother Teresa touches people dying in destitution in Calcutta. A church leader in China resumes his proclamation just days after being let out of prison for the same offense. A widow forgives the drunk driver who took away her husband. A teacher spends hours after school to help one student whose life hangs in the balance. These things happen only by the power of God, and they become the most enduring influence in society. "His divine power has given us everything we need for a godly life" (2 Peter 1:3).

Confronting the Powers

The rise of Adolf Hitler and the Third Reich was as demonic as anything anyone had ever seen in history. As a pastor and theologian, Dietrich Bonhoeffer (1906–45) exercised spiritual influence to the point of paying the ultimate price. In Bonhoeffer's story we understand what it means to "confront the powers."[1]

On February 1, 1933, Bonhoeffer was just twenty-six years old when he delivered an address that repudiated the Führer principle. He sat at a microphone in a radio studio in Berlin two days after Hitler was appointed chancellor of the German Republic and uncovered the corrupt idea of Führer (leader), warning that leadership as strong-armed power would lead to rule by Verführer (mis-leader, seducer).[2] Bonhoeffer had no power by which to confront the powers except truth and persuasion. Later that year he was ordained. In 1934 he helped organize the Confessing Church and signed the Barmen Declaration, which asserted that Christ, not the Führer, is head of the church.

Earlier he had studied theology at Tübingen University and produced a thesis that was a fresh new look at the nature of the church. He spent a year in New York teaching theology and witnessed the vitality of the African American church experience during the period he attended Abyssinian Baptist Church. Later he pastored two small German congregations in England. A brilliant theologian, Bonhoeffer took great care in preparing sermons for the handful of people under his care.

In 1939 he went to America again, but decided almost immediately to return to Germany to do what he could in the gathering storm. The Nazis tried to silence Bonhoeffer by forbidding him to speak in public or to publish.

---

1. For a full telling of the story, see Eric Metaxas, *Bonhoeffer: Pastor, Martyr, Prophet, Spy* (Nashville: Thomas Nelson, 2011).

2. Though the address may not have been directed solely at Hitler at this early stage, it was prophetic of the crisis soon to unfold.

He joined the German resistance and was instrumental in forming the plot to assassinate Hitler. Bonhoeffer was arrested and put in Buchenwald concentration camp, then Regensburg, and finally, Flossenburg. With the Third Reich crumbling and Hitler's defeat imminent, orders were given for Bonhoeffer to be executed, and on April 9, 1945, Bonhoeffer was hanged. For twelve years he had confronted the powers. He did so in sermons and writings, in pastoral ministry, and finally in the extremity of political resistance. What he did in a very short adult life continues to be a powerful influence on people all over the world.

While Hitler idolized power, authority, and his own twisted form of truth, in the end a young German pastor showed that Hitler never had any of it. Bonhoeffer died with wire around his neck but prayed with his fellow prisoners with a peaceful demeanor just minutes before. Three weeks later Hitler died by taking poison and shooting himself after days of insane ravings.

If there is a vacuum of spiritual leadership in a culture, it will be filled with something nefarious. Jesus said, "The thief comes only to steal and kill and destroy," but of himself: "I have come that they may have life, and have it to the full" (John 10:10).

Ephesians 6:12 says, "Our struggle is not against flesh and blood, but against the rulers, against the authorities, against the powers of this dark world and against the spiritual forces of evil in the heavenly realms." Scholarly debates about this and similar passages (e.g., Col. 1:16; 2:15) have centered on whether by "powers" and "authorities" the apostle Paul is referring to spiritual powers or evil human power structures, i.e., totalitarian regimes, social injustice, etc. Or is it that the two intersect? That destructive governments, systems, and rulers that wield power in wanton ways are the earthly manifestation of spiritual powers of evil? For Dietrich Bonhoeffer, there was no question that the two intersect.

Power Today

Human nature does not change. Every generation experiences the power contests: grabbing power, suppressing power, using power constructively, sharing power. The difference today is that the means of having and using power are magnified. We don't just have pockets of wealth today, but enormous centers of wealth. Mass communication capabilities make the power of truth or propaganda many times greater than was the case just a generation ago. Today regimes rise and fall in fits and starts.

So the question is, What does the proper use of power look like in spiritual leadership?

First, we must treat any lust for power in ourselves as a deathly pathology of the soul. We cannot rely on ourselves because power has an intoxicating effect. Every leader should have trusted friends and colleagues who will honestly flag the least hint of power grabbing.

On the other hand, believers must act in the power of the Holy Spirit in carrying out the mission of reconciliation in the world. People whose names we do not know are being prepared today to be the next Dietrich Bonhoeffer or Billy Graham or William Wilberforce. But perhaps we should not focus too much on the extraordinary cases. Everyone who exercises spiritual leadership needs to desire to be an instrument of the Holy Spirit, who works powerfully in us. A Christian teacher may have to stand up to an abusive parent, a youth pastor may have to confront a student who has become captivated with the occult, a business owner may have to decide whether to bring a lawsuit against an unscrupulous partner. Office managers need to decide what to do with power differentials in the workplace. A believer who has a strong desire to run for political office needs to decide on his ethical standards before he ever begins. An accountability group leader needs to determine what kind of expectations to have in the group. There are innumerable ways any of us may be called upon to connect the power of the Spirit with everyday needs.

Finally, it is important to stay focused on the real source of power, which is the message about divine restoration. With Paul we can say: "I am not ashamed of the gospel, because it is the power of God that brings salvation to everyone who believes" (Rom. 1:16). When we need power to do the task at hand, to construct new initiatives, or to manage unmanageable situations, there is no greater power than the reality and message that in Christ, God has begun a radical work of restoration in the human race. This gospel says that God has saved, is saving, and will save and restore people. Spiritual leadership draws on a kind of power that surpasses all forms of blunt-edged, push-and-shove, maim-and-kill leadership that is exercised in the world today. The gospel of human restoration in Christ is able to shape institutions, cultures, and history because it begins with this radical re-creation in real men and women.

This message is about Christ and is Christ. This gospel is unambiguous: "Christ the power of God and the wisdom of God" (1 Cor. 1:24). The message is about a present-day trajectory toward a final divine conquest, but not before the decisive judgment of sin. "The message of the cross is foolishness to those who are perishing, but to us who are being saved it is the power of God" (1 Cor. 1:18).

There is power in the spiritual influence exercised by a teacher who knows education is not just information dumping, but life formation. The business leader who wants the gospel to make a difference in his life and career needs to see that the way he conducts himself is a message of hope—and in that is real power. A community leader can get strength from God's commitment to restore human community—and know the power of that. Church leaders can restore their commitment to the gospel and know that, even at a pragmatic level, the gospel really works. People are not transformed by organizational machinery—they are transformed by the power of God when the gospel is the main message.

The real irony is that power can destroy and it can save. It is as true today as ever before: "power corrupts; absolute power corrupts absolutely." Which is why we need the pure restorative power of God applied in every area of life. We are all in the middle of a power struggle. In the midst of it people get hurt. Cross precedes resurrection; sacrifice comes before success.

Chapter 13

ACCEPT AUTHORITY

> Authority poisons everybody who takes authority on himself. — *Vladimir Lenin*

Every person who exercises initiative or influence at some point or another will be challenged by someone who asks, "What right do you have to do that?" The question may be over something you said, or a decision you made, or a course of action you set. But usually it comes up when you do something that impinges on someone else. Most people have these two contradictory desires: wanting to be led, and resisting being told what to do. So even if the question is not asked out loud, people wonder what right other people have to tell them what to do or to think. Those who bristle may keep their mouths shut and hold some resentment, which festers over time, so that relationships become increasingly strained. This is only exacerbated when the influencer senses disgruntled compliance and leads by pushing forward harder. Power itself is not the answer to the question of authority. "Might makes right" worked for medieval kings, but it is hardly a dignified method of spiritual influence.

We should not be surprised when people wonder, What right does that person over there have to try to exercise authority over me?

In a typical work setting the answer is simple: you have the right to make decisions, to set direction, and to tell other people what to do if you have a certain position on the organizational chart and a sign on your office door that identifies your rank. In most settings this is not controversial at all. The Bible makes it clear that God has ordained certain authority structures so that there is order instead of chaos in the world. Romans 13 speaks of God having established civic authority structures. To have police, courts, mayors, governors, magistrates, and other "authorities," as imperfect as they may be, is far better than anarchy.

But that is not enough. We need the order of God. God's influence in fixing a broken world goes by many names: shalom, reconciliation, flourishing, health, justice, order. Things are not the way they are supposed to be, and so God has moved in a decisive way to restore things to their proper order. God has the authority to do so, and he imparts authority to us to do the work.

And so

- a justice ministry seeks to stem the tide of human trafficking, bringing order where disorder has wrecked lives.
- a youth pastor tries to help students live under the protective order of God.
- a business owner starts a job training program to bring order out of the chaos of chronic unemployment.
- a president of a missions organization brings order to what had developed into a tangled mess of projects.
- a newly elected Christian legislator sees an opportunity to enhance law and order to the benefit of the community.

When capable leaders accept a higher authority to carry out a work of restoration in the world, then people reap the benefits that spiritual leadership brings.

Know What Authority Means

Power is the ability to do a thing, while authority is the right to do so. But they are so intertwined that when people are given authority, they gain power right away.

"By what authority are you doing these things?" the religious authorities asked Jesus when they witnessed his miraculous power to heal. They could not deny the power—that was right before their eyes. So they questioned Jesus' right to exercise the power. What a dangerous position to take—standing in the way of what God wants to do because of a specious argument about authority!

Spiritual leadership is not defined by or limited to office. An organization needs clarity about who has the right to make different kinds of decisions, but some of the most creative, transformative, breakthrough initiatives happen because the Spirit moves or inspires someone—whether they have the "office" to do so or not.

Who Has "Spiritual Authority"?

Who has "spiritual authority"? The short answer to the question is: anybody the Spirit chooses to use. This is what makes spiritual influence exciting and dynamic. In human organizations everything runs according to the predetermined structure. (Although many organizations today are learning that freedom to create and innovate—at any level in the organization—may be more important than merely regulating the workforce.) Everything is different when we believe that a vigorous God wants to surprise us by using ordinary people as his extraordinary instruments. God is not limited to organizational charts. You don't need a title to be a leader.

That innovative new outreach idea for a church may come from a pastor with just a couple of years of experience. An administrative assistant may be the person who has the spiritual discernment to see how a bad relationship between two managers is holding back a whole company. A new teacher may experiment with a novel style and see great effects in the classroom. The question is, Are established leaders open enough to learn something new, and to learn it from someone who does not have positional or official authority? If we believe that the Spirit of God may use anybody at any time we have to be open-minded. This is what makes spiritual leadership exciting.

Spiritual authority is sometimes based on office and sometimes on gifting. We need the office of leadership, that is, the defined, delegated, positional right to serve people by bringing them under the influence of God. And so some people will have titles like managing director, senior pastor, or vice president. Meanwhile others will have spiritual authority because God has given them extraordinary character and skill, or creativity, faith, or wisdom. They are the kind of people others naturally follow. Their authority is more natural than official, but is no less authentic.

Spiritual influence extends far beyond those who have official titles, and that is a good thing because we need many people who are helping others come under the transformative influence of God. We don't just need generals—we also need colonels, captains, lieutenants, sergeants, and many foot soldiers who rise to the occasion when leadership is needed. Pharisees and their modern counterparts have a problem with that. They are ever tracking who has office and who does not. They spend much of their time suppressing the efforts of people whom they do not consider bona fide leaders. In a worst-case scenario, they consider regulation their only responsibility and develop a self-righteousness and pride of position that kills the motive of mission. If policy wonks tried to condemn Jesus, they'll try to do it to anybody.

Abuse of Authority

There is no easy antidote for bureaucratic Pharisaism. The forces of control and regulation are powerful and often deeply entrenched. Traditions become sacrosanct because the original motives behind them are typically good: hold to the truth, fend off attacks, be faithful to the cause. But any cause can become an empty shell of what it was originally.

The solution for the fossilization of leadership today lies at the center of the gospel. Jesus shattered the foundations of the spiritual bureaucrats of his day with the kingdom-of-God message. God must reign. God does reign. And God needs no one's permission. His authority is absolute. Our authority is strictly derivative, and only as sound as it is connected with the purposes of God.

This is liberating for people. Spiritual leadership means inspiring people about being part of a movement that is as expansive as the imagination of God and as good as the heart of God.

Earlier we quoted the aphorism "power corrupts; absolute power corrupts absolutely." So it is with authority. Give someone a title of importance, and they will be tempted to focus on position. It is just human nature. The most damaging form of status-seeking may not be the grossly corrupt leaders, but the subtle, deeply buried motives of self-preservation and turf protection that lie in the heart of almost anybody who has been given authority. Authority can be a powerful drug.

When he tempted Jesus, the Evil One led him up to a high place and showed him in an instant all the kingdoms of the world, and then made an offer buried in a lie placed like bait on a hook: "I will give you all their authority and splendor; for it has been given to me, and I can give it to anyone I want to. If you worship me, it will all be yours" (Luke 4:5–6). Evil always claims authority. It always promises power and status. And it always brings down those who take the bait.

"Worship the Lord your God and serve him only" was Jesus' response (Luke 4:8). And worshiping God remains Jesus' antidote for abuses of authority. Worship restores order: God the authority, we the servants. We have authority only as an extension of the call and the work of God.

Acting with Authority

The ministry of the apostle Paul provides a window into the complexities of leading with authority. With his dramatic call to ministry, Paul was given authority. But his authority was continually being questioned. Because he was not one of the twelve original disciples, he was not a "real" apostle like Peter, James, and John, some said. He abused his authority, according to others. His motives were all wrong, some declared. One has to wonder how the man could sleep at night.

And so, when he wrote to the church in Corinth when their relationship was very rocky, he reminded them, "Even if I boast somewhat freely about the authority the Lord gave us for building you up rather than pulling you down, I will not be ashamed of it"

(2 Cor. 10:8). He wrote a stern letter, full of anguish and hurt, and tells them: "This is why I write these things when I am absent, that when I come I may not have to be harsh in my use of authority—the authority the Lord gave me for building you up, not for tearing you down" (2 Cor. 13:10). Paul's courageous faith allowed him to assert authority, and his utter humility kept him from being intoxicated by power.

So here it is: God gives authority (in this case, the right to speak truth into a sick church), but it is kept in proper bounds by right motive. Like any child who feels diminished by discipline, the Corinthian church felt torn down when the apostle was really breaking down difficult problems so that they, as people, could be built up. If Paul was a man abusing authority, he would have sought personal gain in his relationships, and he could have. But instead of getting wealthy and comfortable, he lived a life of hunger, thirst, physical distress, rejection, uncertainty. The onetime Pharisee who had taken authority from the chief priests to put followers of Jesus in prison (Acts 26:10) now worked under the direct authority of God to multiply grace and truth in people's lives.

And so in spiritual influence we are acting with authority because God has granted the right. We don't invent, grab, or presume authority. We accept it—gingerly.

The Issue of Authority Today

Authority is a complicated and controversial subject. In many countries recently, people have risen up against their authoritarian leaders when they realized that their leaders were governing from self-interest, not for the good of the people. In our own country, many people have challenged the authority of religious, political, financial, and business leaders, openly questioning their motives and actions. Where warranted, we should heed and respect that skepticism.

What we need today are leaders who base their authority not on their position or their power but on God's authority. Their motive to wield authority should be that they want to see God's reign extended into people's lives and to transform organizations and institutions.

We do not need people who crave power and authority, but who respectfully accept authority under God's call and delight in God's purposes being accomplished. We need leaders who hope for rewards, not awards. Here are some practical steps toward the proper use of authority.

- We all need defined lines of accountability that include regular dialogue about our activities and priorities with trusted others.
- Candor must be the norm of ongoing conversations between us and those we are accountable to. This includes friends and family.
- Collegial leadership should be common. Even if an organization requires a pyramid hierarchical structure, those who are near the top of the pecking order can still use colleagues and processes, which prevent sudden and arbitrary decision making.
- We need to keep coming back to the mission Christ gave us. Our goal, no matter the setting, must be to bring more people under the benefits of the kingdom of Christ. We are really accomplishing something when we see people come under the beneficent authority of Jesus. His influence is the one that endures.

In the end, the proper use of authority is an act of love and responsibility. Journalist Sebastian Junger lived and moved with a platoon of soldiers in a dangerous part of Afghanistan for over a year. He saw firsthand how dependent the soldiers were on each other and how even small things could spell the difference between life and death. In such circumstances anyone might have to be an authoritative influence.

Junger wrote in his book *War*, "Margins were so small and errors potentially so catastrophic that every soldier had a kind of de facto authority to reprimand others — in some cases even officers. And because combat can hinge on [small] details, there was nothing in a soldier's daily routine that fell outside the group's purview. Whether you tied your shoes or cleaned your weapon or drank enough water or secured your night vision gear were all matters of public concern and so were open to public scrutiny."[1]

The more serious the stakes, the more we need authoritative voices that speak the truth. Power, authority, and truth — they're all connected.

---

1. Sebastian Junger, *War* (New York: Twelve, 2010), 160.

Chapter 14

PROMOTE TRUTH

> Truth is so obscure in these times, and falsehood so established, that, unless we love the truth, we cannot know it.
> —*Blaise Pascal*

Power, authority, and truth are the dynamics of God's movement in the world, and the dynamics of influence and leadership. We come now to truth.

Among the highest responsibilities of spiritual leadership is helping people ground their lives in reality. This is what it means to lead people to "the truth." The quest for spiritual truth is not about amassing information; it is to know the way things really are—all things in life—and to be able to live well as a result.

In today's world there are many doubts about truth. Is there any such thing as truth? How can one know that a particular thing is true? Isn't it arrogant for people to say that they know "the truth"? What are we to make of the long history of leaders manipulating others through their claim on truth? How can anyone trust leaders who have violated the truth? Are politicians fully truthful in anything they say? What should we make of preachers who seem to have flights of fancy with little grounding in the truth? When should we believe a leader who asks us to believe a certain truth?

Add to that today's confusing messages. Which website's information is reliable? Which cable news program is biased in reporting the news? Is there a unity of biblical truth? Why are there so many denominations?

If Jesus had to say over and over again, "I tell you the truth," it should come as no surprise that we need to as well. We cannot assume that people will believe what we are saying. Not even when we preface it with "truly," "really," "honestly." And that is a good thing. Only God is the Truth; we know truth and communicate truth only through the imperfect lenses of our lives. Influencers who have followers who believe everything they say all the time have merely managed to get lemmings to follow.

Truth is so much more than a list of propositions. We like to make lists and categorize, so we tend to think of truths in that way. Knowing the truth in that mindset means collecting an ever-expanding set of theses and arguments. The biblical idea of truth, however, is the total tapestry of reality — as based first in the character of God who is truth. Propositions do matter, but only as they tie into the complete fabric of reality.

Behind it all is God — the ultimate reality. The Old Testament Hebrew concept of truth is the near equivalent of faithfulness. As God is, so is his truth: firm, sure, reliable, verifiable, steadfast, certain, established, trustworthy, indisputable, enduring, everlasting, unchangeable.

Can anyone doubt we need truth today? Everybody needs a firm, reliable, accurate grasp of reality — even if they feel threatened by it.

The Truth We All Need

It is a remarkable privilege to help people live in reality. Jesus' proverb — "you will know the truth, and the truth will set you free" (John 8:32) — is not just a slogan. All truth, even the harshest truths about the hardest realities, when grasped, liberates us from ignorance and self-deception.

We can lead people toward truth in many ways. For example, we might assure someone who is doubting the goodness of God that the sins of people are not God's fault. Or show an agnostic that it really is possible to have confidence in the reality of God. Truth telling may take the form of showing people how to persevere in the face of personal difficulties, preaching a sermon that shows how forgiveness works, or teaching on morality and ethics as the reality of the good life.

As a practical matter, truth telling includes leading an honest evaluation of the strengths and weaknesses of an organization, a process which makes real improvements possible. Truth telling also calls a leader to admit mistakes and shortcomings instead of flaunting a false persona.

Getting grounded in reality by learning and accepting the truth is an endless process. But the rewards are enormous.

Renewing Our Confidence

We have a deposit of truth in the Holy Scriptures. Because we never arrive at a permanent state of trust in biblical truth, we need to keep renewing our confidence. Knowing the truth is a relationship, because it means knowing God. And relationships are not static. The strongest believers of the Bible need to make sure their hearts remain soft to the impress of God. The Pharisees prided themselves on biblical knowledge, and they did have a remarkable proficiency with the letter of the law. But Jesus said to them, "You do not know the Scriptures or the power of God" (Matt. 22:29). Knowing is more than memorizing. Truth is bigger than words.

Christian leaders have had a clumsy relationship with the Word of God. We have alternated between nonscriptural pragmatic ideas of leadership to Bible-pounding legalism or contorted proof texting—neither of which is acceptable. Or we have kept the theology and the practicalities of leadership separated. The real power of spiritual influence comes through when the substance of Scripture continually shapes our attitudes, values, and opinions. This does not mean artificially quoting chapter and verse for everything we do, which just comes off as disingenuous and can model the wrong use of Scripture.

But one of the most important reasons to be continually renewed and enlightened by God's Word is that then our enthusiasm for

God's truth will be infectious. One of the best ways to help people get captivated by the truth of God is for us to show ourselves to be so captivated—to show that we are attracted to, held by, carried off by, enraptured with, engrossed by the truth we ourselves are discovering about God and the reality of the world we live in. There is an excellent precedent for this in Martin Luther's bold statement as he stood before the assembly at Worms: "My conscience is held captive by the Word of God."

We can influence people for the good when we speak of our own enthusiasm for the influence of the Word of God in our lives. That we cannot imagine living any other way. That we can't wait for the next lesson. That we're eager to share what we are learning. That we long to see as many people as possible running toward that place where the river of God's truth flows.

Clearly, one of the most important disciplines for spiritual influence is the regular, thoughtful reading and study of Scripture. Our minds must be filled with Scripture and shaped by Scripture. Our instincts must be trained so that in a split second, when we are called upon to react, our feet are already steadied on the foundation of God's truth expressed in Scripture.

Our leadership is in the thirst. It is the thirst. "As the deer pants for streams of water, so my soul pants for you, my God. My soul thirsts for God, for the living God" (Ps. 42:1–2). Influence in; influence out.

Improving Communication Skills

Spiritual leadership today requires that we continually hone our ability to communicate biblical truth. As the language of our times changes, so must our ways of explaining the timeless truth of Scripture.

We need to use every means of communication available to us. Today that includes writing, whether that be letters, blogs, books, opt-in email newsletters, or other forms. Some influencers have the ability to use social media in ways that are authentic and personal; and there is no more direct form of communication than intentional one-on-one conversations. We need to save time for spontaneous free-form conversations.

Public speaking is an extraordinary opportunity for spiritual influence. Whether the occasion is giving a brief devotional, a training seminar, a lecture, or a sermon, there are objective standards that will help our effectiveness in public speaking.

1. Take any opportunity you have to speak in front of a group as a high priority. It is a chance for you to plant in the minds and hearts of others seeds of God's grace and truth, which can be a turning point.

2. Avoid clichés when explaining biblical truth. They are a superficial and lazy way of communicating.

3. Think of memorable turns of phrase that will stick in people's minds.

4. Speak with clarity. Have a single main point. Your listeners should be able to answer the question, What was that talk about?

5. Illustrate the truth with real-life examples. Avoid cute analogies. Don't quote movies others will never see.

6. Be authentic, but not artificially so. Perceptive people can sense a preplanned "authenticity" point in a talk. Moments of vulnerability can become routine. Just be yourself. Be honest.

7. Make biblical truth the foundation of your talk.

8. Study thoroughly. Prepare well. You gain immediate credibility with your audience if they sense that you care enough about them to have invested your time in preparation. Filling time by speaking off the cuff is only impressive to the speaker.

9. Respect other people's time. Do not go over your allotted time limit, which is simply lack of discipline. Never use the excuse that you need more time to communicate your given topic (a habit many speakers often repeat!). Something valuable can be said about any topic in whatever time parameters you have been given. You have the assignment. You have the control. Model careful thought and discipline.

10. Read people's faces. They are "talking" back to you as you speak to them. Dialogues are better than monologues. If their eyeballs are rolling back in their sockets, step up the energy, not just by upping your volume, but by changing the content.

11. Make it your aim to address head, heart, and will. Head: provide a new insight. Heart: go deep. Will: point to action and response. The purpose of some talks may be more of one of these than the others, but most talks can do all three.

12. Make it matter to them because it matters to you. If you aren't gripped by the truth you are communicating, you cannot expect it to be compelling to others. Cancel the talk. Or pray for a sense of conviction.

13. If you talk to a particular group on a regular basis, take a long view. Start a fire and keep it going. Don't look at any one talk as one chance to produce a fireworks display.

The bottom line is this: respect God's truth, and respect the people you are speaking to. Being a herald is an act of love. Turn influence into spiritual influence by letting the truth flow to you and then flow through you. Relish the fact that it is not your truth, but God's.

A Voice of Truth

One day *New York Times* columnist David Brooks wrote a piece called "Who Is John Stott?" Brooks was bemoaning the fact that the media always choose the wrong people to represent evangelical Christianity, putting the microphone in front of people who are, in his opinion, "buffoons." If reporters were smart, Brooks said, they'd look to John R. W. Stott as the voice of evangelical Christianity. It is a voice that is "friendly, courteous and natural. It is humble and self-critical, but also confident, joyful and optimistic." Brooks went on to reflect on why this evangelical preacher is so compelling to him, a Jew. It has to do with Stott's uncompromising "thoughtful allegiance to scripture." Brooks concluded, "Most important, he does not believe truth is plural. He does not believe in relativizing good and evil or that all faiths are independently valid, or that truth is something humans are working toward. Instead, Truth has been revealed."[1]

John Stott was a pastor in London for many years and gradually became a friend to dozens of countries he visited in his itinerant speaking ministry. He was driven by his conviction that the truth of God in Christ is at the core of the mission that believers share. He never flaunted the fact that he served as chaplain to the Queen of England, nor did he bask in the multitudes of accolades he received. He lived as simply as possible, wrote books in a simple cottage in Wales, never married, and was called "Uncle John" by hundreds of younger people to whom he was mentor.

Stott always stood erect at the podium from which he spoke, turning small-sized pages in a notebook to march steadily through his talk. He did not walk around. Hardly gestured. But in his voice was a firm conviction that punctuated every word and phrase. Sacrifice, truth, crucifixion, mission, world, redemption—and especially, Christ. He did not arrest your attention with fancy illustrations, but with the substance of the truth. He did not speak on topics, but about reality. The orderliness of his analysis showed respect toward his listeners. An authentic longing to help people. And underlying it all was an irenic spirit. He was polite not because he was an Englishman, but because the grace of Christ required it. Grace and peace—the key words of Pauline salutations—were the values that opened the door of credibility to untold thousands of people.

Stott demonstrated spiritual influence not primarily because he built an organization or led an institution. He led by planting the seeds of truth—widely, deeply, continually, over a period of decades. In John Stott's final public address he raised the question, What are we trying to do in the mission? In his mind the answer was unambiguous: to help people become more like Christ.

The core elements of Stott's influence by truth telling are within our grasp immediately. We must

- Make personal devotion to God in Christ our highest priority.

1. David Brooks, "Who Is John Stott?" *New York Times*, November 30, 2004, http://www.nytimes.com/2004/11/30/opinion/30brooks.html.

- Live consistently, with integrity. Resist the temptation to develop a public persona.
- Develop core disciplines like Scripture reading and meditation, prayer, work, and rest.
- Trust in the unchangeable truth of Scripture. Go deep in our study of it.
- Prepare public talks with a focus on substance. Look for the connections and order of our ideas.
- Value relationships with other leaders. Be a mentor without having to be called a mentor. Follow natural patterns. Don't turn discipleship into a program.
- "Read" the truth of God written in the natural world. Stott was an avid ornithologist (bird watcher). His cumulative knowledge made him a world expert. This was both an avocation and an act of worship. Like many other Christian leaders, Stott practiced a full awareness of God's presence and work, and that included participating in the creation, cultivating a sense of awe and wonder.

Truth Telling Today

Amid the ongoing philosophical debates about the nature of truth, we must not lose our footing when it comes to serving people's real needs. Spiritual leadership is an opportunity to lead people to truth, grounding their lives in reality. Truth is what people need.

In the twenty-first century we need to understand how people receive, test, and assimilate truth.

First, as often as possible we should view truth telling as dialogue. It is not a bad thing that people do not want just to be talked at. They want to talk back, even if that only means a preacher reading the faces of those he is talking to and being responsive to them. People love interviews — to read them, to watch them on television, to follow them on the internet. There is something dynamic about pursuing the truth as a back-and-forth dialogue.

The ancient Greeks used the Socratic method of debate and dialogue as a way of sharpening critical thinking. Thomas Aquinas wrote his massive theology as a series of questions and answers. And the list goes on. Truth telling as dialogue is not a new way or an old way, but a classic way of sharpening one's understanding of reality.

At a practical level that means making classes and training sessions interactive. It means preachers should read the faces of their audiences. We should use the new media as a way of conversation. This does not negate the simple, straight-out proclamation of the truth of God, which includes the prophetic "this is what God says." The question is, What happens next?

Second, we should all be translators of the Word of God. Quoting Scripture is fine, but in today's world people need explanation and incarnation. They need people who have a deep grasp of the truth of God to put it in everyday language, not just repeated clichés. One of the best ways of doing that is to find those genres of Scripture that carry over the easiest for the people we are helping. In some cultures proverbs are easy to grasp. Some are ready to hear the narrative of the life of Jesus. Many people are responsive to the parables of Jesus explained in everyday language. Need to explain salvation to someone? The parable of the prodigal son has it all.

Third, we should show a confidence in the truth. Many people today have gotten jaded and cynical. There is hardly a leader anywhere they trust. As a consequence they give no credence to leaders, and they stop looking for a body of truth that could form a structure for life. They dismiss anybody who even attempts to offer a proposal for a truth-based life.

When talking about truth is a dead-end street, the alternative is to live the truth—which is what we should be doing anyway. Living the truth is how we should understand sexual ethics, money management, and office conversation. Living the truth should affect the way we talk about politics and politicians, world history, and theories about the future. And confidence in the truth—certainty without arrogance—may be the lifeline that we offer people looking for healthy spiritual influence in their lives.

In the past six chapters we have looked at going deep. Spiritual influence—because it deals with human nature at the core—means we must develop discernment, stream wisdom, and think deeply. We need to act and react very carefully in the nexus where divine leadership and human leadership powerfully connect: receiving power, accepting authority, and promoting truth.

It is natural for us to wonder how far our influence can go, but if we want to see an enduring influence we will ask how deep it is going. At the most superficial level some leaders move people around like herding cattle. They are not trying for anything deeper because they don't care about anything deeper. Their objective is simply to get people to do things: go to a place, buy a product, sign up, attend a meeting, donate some money.

A deeper form of leadership probes beneath the surface of things. It seeks to understand motivations, values, and identity. It is leadership by influence, tapping into the deep currents of the influence of God. The deepest form of influence recognizes the spiritual nature of human beings and seeks to impact people, groups, and organizations in that core place where real change happens. This leadership accounts for the deep things that flow from God and can flow to others through us.

These are the kinds of choices we make: Merely sell a product, or spread a resource that promotes human flourishing? Get bodies in a room, or develop community? Become famous, or be influential? Cause people to admire you, or lead them to cherish God?

Part 4

FACING CHALLENGES

Chapter 15

MANAGE EXPECTATIONS

*Don't live down to expectations. Go out there and do
something remarkable.* — Wendy Wasserstein

Six months ago Tom moved almost a thousand miles for a new job
that appeared to be the ideal fit for his abilities, training, and inter-
ests. The interviews had gone well. The timing was right. The com-
pensation was fine. But six months in Tom was feeling tense about his
work, and even more so, about his relationships with both his superi-
ors and the people who reported to him. Everything still looked fine
on paper—it was the unwritten subtleties that were the challenge,
in particular, the expectations coming at him from above and below.

Tom's boss was quick to correct him when he did something
wrong, but was always vague about what he was doing right. It was
uncomfortable to ask the boss for feedback and evaluation because it
felt like he was seeking approval, but he honestly didn't know whether
he was on track or not. He was also wrestling with the expectations
of the people who reported to him. Each person was so different in
what he or she wanted: one was always insecure and looking for affirmation; another was cocky and kept a safe distance. Those who had
worked there for many years seemed to be scrutinizing Tom's every
move, almost as if they were deciding whether he would pass muster

with them. One person was in a family crisis and frequently missed work. Another kept coming to him with personal problems looking for counsel that had nothing to do with the workplace.

When he lay his head on the pillow at night and closed his eyes, Tom saw the faces of his boss and his team staring at him, waiting for him to say something that they would approve of. Tom realized that much of this was in his imagination, and that if he didn't figure out a way of managing the expectations of people, he was going to fail in his work.

The title of this chapter could be misleading. We cannot really manage expectations. That is, we cannot ultimately control the expectations others have of us, nor should it be our highest priority. No matter how hard we try, all the people around us have their own personal reasons why they expect certain things of us, or have too small of expectations. A leader can get exhausted trying to manage the expectations of others: watching, listening, reacting, explaining, apologizing, dancing, measuring, eavesdropping, probing, apologizing again, dancing again. Jumping through hoops—large ones, small ones, sometimes high, sometimes low, sometimes flaming.

Playing to the expectations of others can drain our best energy and distract our attention. The problem is, all the different people who have expectations of a leader do not know about the expectations other people have of the same leader. They just know what they want, and are typically oblivious to the push and pull coming from other corners. Worst of all, we might miss the most important thing—God's expectations of us.

On the other hand, every leader is accountable to someone. We should not think we can or should dodge all expectations. If we don't have proper and reasonable lines of accountability, then our only guide will be the expectations we put on ourselves, and we should not trust ourselves that much.

Why Expectations Are Complicated

Here are some of the reasons we struggle with the issue of expectations.

The people we serve or lead have expectations that often are subjective. They see us from their perspective, which is always a partial viewpoint. A spouse has certain expectations, which will be different from what children expect. The boss has certain expectations, which may be very different from those of the previous boss or the one after. The constituencies we serve have many possible expectations, and there are subgroups of those constituencies that vary greatly in what they expect. Everybody in our lives has a conviction, in other words, about who we should be and what we should do. We cannot hope to please them all in the same way.

Expectations are often arbitrary, emerging from mere opinion or whim. Most people have opinions just because they have opinions. All opinions are judgments, even though we don't view it that way when we speak up. The visibility of leaders means that they are under a continual barrage of judgments.

Expectations are reciprocal. Leaders have to deal with the expectations of others, while they themselves are imposing expectations on others, because that is part of the task. If we are subjective and arbitrary in the expectations we impose on others, we can hardly complain when others impose expectations on us. The solution is to strive in every way possible to discern what God expects, and communicate that to the people we lead. Spiritual leadership can save us, in other words, from entanglements over control, because the objective is always to discern the will of God. Nothing else matters.

People assume they have the right to have expectations. Only very mature people are deliberate about the expectations they have of others. They think through what is reasonable, they seek to understand the other person, and they do not assume they necessarily even have a right to impose expectations. How much easier life would be if we stopped playing God in our evaluations and expectations of others! This kind of wisdom is rare. It is generous and forbearing. More often, people look at each other with the attitude: "What have you done for me lately?" And they are not even aware that they are being presumptuous. They just scan and scrutinize, weigh and measure — and then talk indiscreetly to others about their evaluations.

The roots of expectations go deeply into culture. Most people do not reflect on the expectations they have of others; they just expect.

And most people don't realize their expectations are typically defined by what is normal for them in their culture. Japanese managers have very different expectations from managers of organizations in France. The expectations placed on public school teachers can be different from those placed on private school teachers. Pastors of smaller churches run into different expectations than those experienced by megachurch pastors (and the smaller setting does not necessarily mean expectations that are easier to satisfy).

Expectations are also rooted in our personal learned patterns of life. The person who grew up with one or two controlling parents may react by throwing off all expectations they have of others, or by becoming high-control people themselves, passing on the same bitter pill they had to swallow.

Managing expectations is a challenge! Thus, the old adage: "A leader must have the mind of a scholar, the heart of a child, and the skin of a rhinoceros." Some leaders have to deal with the expectations of ten people, others a hundred, thousands, or, for national leaders, millions. These forces are strong. We are always having to walk the fine line between being overly sensitive to expectations and being uncaring or callous.

Turning Expectations Upside Down

Too often life is a relentless push and pull of expectations and control. Some influencers think that the sum total of their job is to control, and to impose expectations accordingly. Wiser people know that a higher aim is to motivate people toward accomplishments that are a match for who they are. But the wisest influencers believe it is their duty to help people live up to the calling of God and the expectations God places before them. This is a complete reversal of the normal dynamics of expectations. It is to go from "What have you done for me lately?" to "What does God really want you to do, going forward?" People who are committed to the call from heaven do the most good on earth. When we guide people toward God's will, not our will, they will have a higher motivation to do the task at hand thoroughly, reliably, and effectively. When people work just to please the boss, the fulfillment never gets any higher than the boss's imagination. When they work in a way that pleases God, the result can exceed all expectations.

But how do we do that? How do we turn expectations upside down so that we are all aiming solely at God's expectations, without being artificially superspiritual?

What do we do with the reality that some people expect too much of us, others too little, and others simply expect the wrong things? Adjusting expectations is a necessary and continual process. Here are some ways we can do that.

Periodically let people know what you believe God wants you to do. This assumes, of course, that you have done everything in your power to discern what that is. You've searched your heart, prayed, read Scripture, sought the counsel of wise people, conversed with people you are accountable to and gotten affirmation from them, sized up your lifestyle, and so on. So you come to the people you are trying to influence and you tell them what your aims are, and something of the process of how you got there. In so doing, you're modeling for others how they can think through their own priorities.

Underpromise and overdeliver. There are few things more discouraging for people than leaders who make promises, spout big talk, get people enthused—and then don't deliver. As the aphorism goes: "The road to hell is paved with good intentions." Wise influencers resist the temptation to get people pumped up with big talk (as if that in itself ever accomplishes anything). They promise only what they can deliver, and then they try to deliver double what they promised in the first place. It is remarkable how people respond when they get from their leaders more than they were expecting.

Respond in a timely way. If you are not able to respond to emails, say so. If you cannot attend an appreciation brunch, send your regrets immediately. Never ignore an RSVP (remember what RSVP means: *répondez s'il vous plaît*, "please respond"). To say "no" is not disrespect; ignoring people is.

Tell people what not to expect. If you tell people that there are a dozen different things you could do, but you know that there are three main things you should do, and so you will be focusing on them, people will usually understand. People respect intentionality. This assumes, of course, that you are not merely focusing on what you enjoy or what comes easy for you.

Adapt and communicate. God's expectations of us will change over time. We need to review our stance on a regular basis. And when we adjust the priorities of our work, we need to communicate that to the people we are influencing so that they are neither confused nor frustrated that things have been rearranged and no one told them.

Work through the issue of expectations with your family. One of the greatest points of tension we will face is the push and pull between one's work and one's family life. This issue requires continual management. And all the issues need to be on the table. We need to develop and then attend to the expectations of our family members. We have a scriptural mandate to care for our households, because neglect will invalidate any influence we exercise outside the family (Titus 1:6; 1 Tim. 3:4–5). It is fair for families to say: We know that your work is demanding, and we know that the issues you deal with may always be on your mind, but as much as is humanly possible, when you are with us, be with us. Don't just give us your body while your mind is in an entirely different place.

What Does God Require?

The only expectations that matter, ultimately, are God's expectations. If we live up to those, with God's help, we will be fulfilling all reasonable expectations others have. But before we think of all the small pragmatic priorities we have to focus on, we must begin with global expectations. As the prophet Micah said, "He has shown you, O mortal, what is good. And what does the LORD require of you? To act justly and to love mercy and to walk humbly with your God" (Micah 6:8). God has shown us what is good. He has not left us in the dark. We don't need to invent or reinvent the mission of God. The beginning of all things (Genesis 1) is "good" and "very good." The end of all things is a new creation in which God makes all things new. In between, spiritual influence must focus on what the all-good God calls good. He "requires" these things not just by fiat, but because this is specifically how God restores the world to its proper order.

We looked at Micah 6:8 in an earlier chapter, but let's apply it to the issue of God's expectations:

To act justly. The word *justice* appears over four hundred times in the Old Testament. Justice is when things are right, or when they are set right. Justice is the act of confronting chaos and bringing order. That means advocating for people who are oppressed or are being taken advantage of, teaching about the God-ordered life, counseling people whose lives are in disarray, guiding people who are morally confused, analyzing inequities, promoting fairness. Justice is peace, security, and life. The application for leaders is simple: act justly. That means doing it, not just talking about it. People are inspired when they see leaders who are driven by a sense of justice and who respect the requirements of justice for themselves. They especially appreciate those who are fair-minded and even-handed. They are looking for people bold enough to be advocates for justice.

To love mercy. The Hebrew word *hesed* is translated into English as mercy, love, kindness, grace. It is a central description of the nature of God in the Old Testament. "The LORD, the LORD, the compassionate and gracious God, slow to anger, abounding in love and faithfulness, maintaining love to thousands, and forgiving wickedness, rebellion and sin. Yet he does not leave the guilty unpunished" (Exod. 34:6–7). If we follow God's expectations at this point we will forbear and forgive the failings and foibles of family members, raise our kids with mercy (along with justice), give people a second chance, respond to disadvantaged people who need an advocate. But Micah 6:8 goes beyond occasional acts of mercy; it speaks of "loving mercy." We need to go looking for opportunities to show mercy, not just deliberate when a need arises. Now, there are some people who will warn us not to be too merciful. They're concerned that we will be weak, or will foster dependency, or get our eyes off the work that needs to be done. But the work is this: do justice, love mercy. It is impossible to be too merciful if we are fully committed to justice. Justice prevents mercy from becoming permissiveness (which is really just moral laziness). And mercy makes justice human, keeping it rooted in God's grace-filled nature.

To walk humbly with God. Spiritual influence cannot happen without humility. This small phrase — to walk humbly with God — offers a great picture of the meaning of humility. It is a walk — that is, a lifestyle, a posture, and a forward movement. As a "walk," humility is a continual string of opportunities in life. Every attitude, every decision, every conversation. Every relationship, every email, every purchase. And humility is defined by relationship with God — to walk humbly with God. There is a wonderful clarity here: if we walk with God, that is, with a steady awareness of God's presence and authority over every area of life, then we have every reason not to pretend that we are God — and that is exactly what humility is. Humility includes admitting mistakes and sins, but it is more than that. Humility means living as the creatures we were created to be. If humankind had never sinned, it would still have to be humble. When we walk humbly with God, we are simply being what we are.

In the end, it is possible to exceed the expectations other people have of us — but we get there only by being obsessed with the expectations God has of us.

Chapter 16

PERSEVERE
AND PLOD

God knows our situation; he will not judge us as if we
had no difficulties to overcome. What matters is the sin-
cerity and perseverance of our will to overcome them.
—*C. S. Lewis*

It was a bright early afternoon in the desert of northern Chile and
everything was normal when deep underground disaster happened.
Thirty-three miners were 2,300 feet under the surface of the earth,
three miles in through the winding mine ramps, when the mine
shaft collapsed. No one knew whether the miners had survived or
not. Seventeen days later a probe inserted into the cavity of the mine
was pulled out and a note was attached: "We are well . . . The 33."

The sobering reality of the situation was that, even if the mining
company began drilling an escape shaft for the miners, the process
would take not days or weeks, but months. The men had several days
of emergency food and water. The situation seemed hopeless. But
doing nothing was not an option. The mining company began drilling six-inch holes large enough to let water and food down into the
cavern—and then began to assemble the large equipment to begin
drilling a hole just wide enough for a twenty-one-inch-wide capsule to be lowered to the men. It was estimated that this large-bore

drilling would take months to reach the miners. Months. The experts on the surface knew it; the men living in the stale air and absolute black so far underground knew it.

The way the rescuers worked was to drill rock. Inch by inch. Day by day. The way the miners survived was by living one day at a time, though "days" in the blackness had no measure. They held together as a group, dividing responsibilities between them. One miner, Luis Urzua, quickly emerged as the leader of the group. His cool head and good humor kept the men in decent spirits and their minds on the tasks of survival. He later credited majority decision making for keeping the morale strong. "You just have to speak the truth and believe in democracy," he said.

A full sixty-nine days after the mine collapsed, all thirty-three miners were extracted, one by one, in a small cramped capsule. The crisis began in early August. Now it was early October. They could not have survived physically if they had not persevered spiritually. During those weeks they held chapel services underground. They had crosses, Bibles, and other devotional articles sent down to them. Virtually all of them saw their rescue as an act of God. But they had to wait—so many days, so many weeks—and persevere.

We don't seem to use the word *perseverance* very often. Maybe because it has the word *severe* in it. Or maybe it seems a bit old-fashioned, like King James Bible English. There is no question that other words roll more easily off the tongue, like *winning, succeeding, finishing*. But here it is, the biblical mandate: persevere.

The best influencers know how to persevere. Whether or not they know the duration of the effort, the struggles ahead, the distance to the finish line—or even whether there is a finish line—they keep going. One foot in front of the other. Progressing one inch at a time. Each day a new opportunity to start again. People who persevere hold to a conviction that plodding ahead pleases God, even when there is no applause and no immediate reward.

Modeling perseverance is one of the most powerful forms of spiritual leadership. People look to those who keep going in the face of adversity, who keep faith when they are disappointed in life, who keep their integrity when they are mistreated. Why? Because most people at some time or another plead, "Someone out there, please show me how I can get through." The people who persevere are the influencers, the real leaders, even if they don't have a formal leadership title.

Most of us have stubbed our toe on the famous line at the beginning of the epistle of James: "Consider it pure joy, my brothers and sisters, whenever you face trials of many kinds" (James 1:2). It would seem reasonable that Scripture would associate faith and courage with difficulties—but joy? Pure joy?

We undercut joy in our lives if we think it is the same thing as pleasure or happiness. Joy is not the same thing as enjoyment. Joy keeps a parent plodding ahead during the challenging years of a child's maturing, even when the enjoyment comes in brief spurts. Joy comes from a deep inner conviction that doing the thing you do—teaching, mentoring, managing an organization, leading a small group—is right in God's eyes, is the right fit for your abilities, and is worthwhile even if it takes a long time to accumulate accomplishments. But that's okay because the best accomplishments are built slowly and deliberately. Temples don't spring up overnight. There is no prefabrication in the work of God. Joy is able to meet trials head-on because it gives hope in the face of the trials.

James tells us to "consider it pure joy, my brothers and sisters, whenever you face trials of many kinds, because you know that the testing of your faith produces perseverance. Let perseverance finish its work so that you may be mature and complete, not lacking anything" (James 1:2–4).

Trials produce character. That is, if we persevere through the trials. If at the moment things get difficult, we divert from the proper goal or turn around and run the other way, then not only have we abandoned the work, but we have lost the opportunity to grow as leaders. We need resistance, we need the sparks to fly and the gears to grind once in a while. The only way we change the status quo is to make some messes. Now, sometimes resistance does mean it is time to change direction. Perseverance is not merely stubbornness, however, nor pushing against a brick wall. It is staying on course when we know it is the right course, though difficult.

Perseverance is constancy, endurance, steadfastness, stickability, staying power. The objective of perseverance is hope, the vehicle is faith, and the motive is love. That famous triad in 1 Corinthians 13 (and other passages) is called the things that "remain" (1 Cor. 13:13). Love "always protects, always trusts, always hopes, always perseveres" (13:7).

There are reasons—sometimes life-or-death reasons—why we must exercise the skill of perseverance. We simply must. There are some circumstances in which God wants to do one main thing through a leader—to persevere. To help other people not give up because they see a leader who will not give up.

The word *trial* in this passage of James, repeated elsewhere in the New Testament, is a neutral word. Depending on the context in which it is used, it can mean a difficulty that someone is using to trip someone up (so "temptation") or a challenge that is an opportunity to prevail over (so "test"). The Evil One tempts; God tests. And oftentimes, when we are in the middle of trials, we do not know which it is. And there is no time to try to figure it out. Pushing ahead and enduring is the order of the day.

Why do some people persevere where others throw up their hands and quit?

The courage to persevere comes from an immovable conviction that one's purpose is right and that God is behind it. This conviction must be held with humility, however, because once in a while our convictions are misplaced.

We are able to persevere when we are aiming at long-term, not short-term, rewards. Any effort can surge ahead at one point or drop off significantly. Wars are won by persevering through lost battles. When we know that the end goal is a good one, and when we are realistic about the rise and fall of the journey to get there, we can keep moving ahead.

Our best chance at persevering is when the true horizon we are focused on is heaven itself. This is not just theory or cliché. We really can have an entirely different quality of life and influence if our deepest longing is to one day hear from Jesus: "Well done, good and faithful servant." The question of the day is not whether we have our sights set too low or too high in terms of our goals. There is only one line of sight that will bring order to all our life and work: a vision of Christ seated at the right hand of God the Father, ruling with all justice and mercy. Our influence only means something if it is plotted along that trajectory, and our work ultimately leads people to that same goal.

We are more likely to persevere when we fully believe in the sovereignty of God. It is a comfort to know that God is not shaken by our mistakes, but it is just as important to remember that God is not impressed with our success. God knows our capabilities, because God made us. God knows that on some days we will succeed, and on other days we will fail.

We are more likely to persevere when we are not waiting for adulation, congratulation, or promotion. The moment we focus on impressing others, our attention is diverted from the faithful completion of the task at hand.

We will persevere when we take things one day at a time — especially when we're in a season of severe testing. God doesn't want us to live in the past, and it is impossible to live in the future. The present moment is where we can lay out options and choose the ones that will make this one day productive and good.

"I Can Plod"

William Carey began his barrier-breaking mission work in India in 1798 with enthusiasm. It took perseverance to build cultural connections where nobody had before. To learn indigenous languages, write and print grammars and dictionaries, translate the Bible into Sanskrit.

In a single day, March 11, 1812, the years of work vanished. A fire in Carey's print shop consumed his entire library, including his completed Sanskrit dictionary, part of his Bengal dictionary, two grammar books, and ten translations of the Bible. Also lost were a large supply of English paper, dictionaries, deeds, and account books. Seventeen years of work were taken away. The core accomplishments of the mission were just gone.

Years earlier, William Carey tried to explain to his skeptical father that he had something constructive to do in faraway India. No one had done this kind of work before, which is why Carey is called "the father of modern missions." He couldn't tell his father at that time that he could practice medicine, because he wasn't a doctor. Couldn't say that he'd serve India's political needs, because he had no skill in civil affairs. But Carey knew one thing about himself that was rooted in his personal ordinariness. He said of himself: "I can plod."

After the fire Carey knew what needed to be done. Despite the heartache and discouragement, he knew that he and his fellow workers could retrace their steps and start with page one of the dictionary, the grammars, and the Bible translations. Page two after that. And the trajectory was set. Carey said that it was easier to walk a road the second time—and that is just what they did. It took years, but he re-created what the fire had stolen. By the end of Carey's life, the Bible had been produced in whole or in part in forty-four different languages.

He could plod, and he did plod. One foot in front of the other; one page after another.

Hardly any of us would list in our credentials: I can plod. No one in a job interview today, when asked about his or her capabilities, would say to the boss, "Well, I can plod." The word sounds a bit thick and ugly even when we say it.

Yet by any fair reading of Scripture, the greatest leaders were plodders. Moses on a decades-long march. David fleeing his enemies, hiding in caves. Jesus walking from one village to the next. Paul making long, looping journeys, continually facing the same jealousies, criticism, and skepticism—mostly from his fellow Christian leaders.

It is the plodders who make things happen. They have faced "trials of many kinds." And when they learned perseverance by not giving up, they were stronger, wiser, and more energized than before to keep their eyes on the right horizon.

Here is the secret of plodding, or persevering: you have faith that if today you take just one step in the right trajectory, you have done something constructive, and God is pleased with it.

"You know that the testing of your faith produces perseverance. Let perseverance finish its work so that you may be mature and complete, not lacking anything" (James 1:3–4).

Perseverance Today

Our culture today values quick results over perseverance (which, in the end, drastically weakens culture). People fall for the allure of lotteries and pyramid schemes. Athletes take steroids, students abuse amphetamines, fast food replaces dining. We equate internet searches with serious research. In business people aim at short-term rather than long-term gains. Political leaders don't even think of starting to solve problems that will take thirty years of work when those are exactly the problems we most need them to work on.

Spiritual influence is a countercultural movement today because it assumes that the best growth is organic and progressive. Discipleship develops over time; character forms in response to hundreds of different encounters; knowledge of God doesn't jump off a Wikipedia page.

In spiritual influence, we are challenging people in many ways to slow down, let truth percolate, develop many relationships that will yield many different insights. This does not mean slowness or sluggishness, but deliberateness.

Perseverance is long-view vision. The best work we can do is so important, so big, so visionary, that it cannot be completed in a lifetime. These are the entrepreneurs who start companies that they know will take decades to build, the social activists who take on issues like hunger and disease knowing that there is no total solution on the horizon, but that any good thing that can happen today is a good. These are pastors who know that the renovation of the lives of people will never be complete in this life. The very best leaders accept this paradox and tension: I will commit myself today to something that I will never see completed in my lifetime. But why would I want to commit myself to anything less?

The only ultimate goals worth aiming at are those that we cannot complete on our own.

"Now faith is confidence in what we hope for and assurance about what we do not see." That's the striking opening line of Hebrews 11 that then goes on to catalog giants of the faith from the Old Testament. Abraham and the others who are mentioned are characterized as people who persevered, even if the prize was a long ways away, even beyond their lifetime. "All these people were still living by faith when they died. They did not receive the things promised; they only saw them and welcomed them from a distance" (Heb. 11:13).

Sometimes, instead of asking whether our vision is big enough, we should be asking, Is it far enough?

Chapter 17

EXPECT WOUNDS

It is a sign of a perverse and treacherous disposition to wound the good name of another, when he has no opportunity of defending himself.

—*John Calvin*

In the military there is a term for casualties inflicted by one's fellow soldiers. Whether it is stray mortar fire, a mistaken target in an artillery barrage, or just one rifle pointed at the wrong person in the middle of a dust-filled battle, it is the greatest insult of war. It's called "friendly fire." But there is nothing friendly about it at all.

Friendly fire in battle is unintentional wounding from one's comrades. It is a tragedy to have to say it or face it: leaders wound fellow leaders. It would be nice to say it is always unintentional, but sometimes it is worse than that. And even when unintentional, the extreme carelessness with which leaders sometimes talk about other leaders, or the way they treat them, might as well be called intentional. We hide from this reality, we keep mum, we pretend it isn't true. But thousands of leaders quit because they are wounded by their fellow leaders, and still we don't talk about it.

The Worst Kind of Wounds

The apostle Paul was not hesitant in his letters to tell people about his wounds. In one brief passage he lists imprisonments, beatings without number, the infamous thirty-nine lashings five times, ship-wrecked three times, floating in the ocean for a day and a night. Paul faced dangers from robbers, from his countrymen, and from Gentiles. Dangers in the city, in rivers, in the wilderness. And dangers from people claiming to be but who were false in every way. Sleeplessness, hunger, thirst, and exposure to the elements all contributed to his suffering. (See 2 Cor. 11:23–27.)

But for all this list of trials, it seems that Paul was even more deeply wounded by fellow believers. He wrote about leaders who preached out of envy, even maliciously, to cause him distress in prison. There was competition from the very start. Those who thought Paul arrogant, cavalier, or strident actually relished the opportunity to preach while Paul was sidelined. Wounding. Deep wounding.

We can feel the pain and angst coming from Paul in the letter known as 2 Corinthians, one of the most passionate letters in the New Testament. In it Paul writes about the wounding he caused in his first letter as he recommended strong discipline against a man caught in immorality. He talks about his own difficult relationship with some in the Corinthian church. He felt the bite of their criticism—that he was not an eloquent speaker, that he was not one of the "super-apostles" (2 Cor. 12:11). Paul actually admits that he felt afraid to spend time with them because of the surging currents of disapproval there.

Anticipating another visit, he speaks honestly: "I am afraid that when I come I may not find you as I want you to be, and you may not find me as you want me to be. I fear that there may be discord, jealousy, fits of rage, selfish ambition, slander, gossip, arrogance and disorder. I am afraid that when I come again my God will humble me before you, and I will be grieved over many who have sinned earlier and have not repented" (2 Cor. 12:20–21). The man who endured incredible life-threatening physical distress in his life admits that he is afraid to come before critical brothers and sisters. The wounds of fellow believers are powerful.

Paul's relationship with the church of Corinth was tough, full of wounds from start to finish. But at the end of the letter, Paul assumes the best: "May the grace of the Lord Jesus Christ, and the love of God, and the fellowship of the Holy Spirit be with you all" (2 Cor. 13:14). These are not empty words. Paul was in a tough leadership challenge: a local church beset with problems of ethics, morality, theology, and worship. A close but tense relationship with wounds on both sides.

Hold On to God

Paul's approach is honest, open, and practical. He is going to visit the believers in Corinth, and they are going to sit down and try to work things out. He assumes the best but is prepared for the worst. But most important, he leans on God as the leader: the grace of Christ, the love of the Father, the *koinonia* of the Holy Spirit. Live long enough and you will expect wounds. Surviving is possible by holding on to God.

When we are wounded, or when we know we have wounded others — whether the wounds are still bleeding or are in the distant past and are marked by ugly scars — God is our only hope. We don't have enough grace, enough love, and we will not have the desire to close ranks in real fellowship, without God.

The wounding that happens among believers is extremely discouraging. Thousands of church leaders, for instance, quit every year because they become disillusioned with the behavior of fellow believers. People who are highly competitive often do not see that their spiritual ambitions are taking the form of competing against fellow leaders in ways that discredit the cause.

The biases and prejudices that are at the core of who we are often retain leverage over our actions even when we think we're rising above them. It is one thing for a man to say he is not misogynistic; it is another to be rid of any lingering bias against women. It is easy to say that one is not racist, but there are many ways we tend to keep our distance from people of a different race. It is commonplace for leaders to say that they respect those whose work is small and hidden, but our tendency is still to put the spotlight on those whose work is big and splashy.

We may say that there are multiple valid styles of leadership, but subconsciously we often invalidate leaders who do things differently. We may invite onto our team only the people whose style matches our own.

We may say that we believe "when we are weak then we are strong," but we treat the weak or wounded leader as fatally flawed, and look for ways to discard him or her.

It is tragic but true that sometimes we shoot our wounded. Someone gets depleted or depressed, and while there are offers of grace and healing, the wider community nullifies the leader's role. A leader makes a mistake, and others doubt the person's overall competency. It becomes obvious that a leader has a blind spot or lack of awareness, and instead of coming around to him or her to teach, correct, and mentor, people don't bother to take the time.

We live in a disposable age. Disposable cameras, disposable lighters, disposable pens, disposable leaders. We manufacture kitchen appliances with a planned obsolescence of just a few years. We don't want to bother to repair. Just throw the old one out and buy a new one.

Today there is a widespread tendency to think that if things aren't working out, it's best just to find a new leader. It is quick; it's decisive; it's easy (at least at the start). The tragedy is that the whole aim of spiritual leadership is to restore the fallen order to what God intended it to be. God does not create with planned obsolescence, and he does not shoot the wounded. When we simply dispose of people, or take wounds and make them deeper, we betray our call to be agents of healing, reconciliation, and restoration.

Wounding Today

Some cultural trends make us more likely to wound each other. A corporate model of leadership in which the only value is increasing the bottom line will be a cutthroat system. Companies do need to turn a profit, but the the value system certainly can be broadened beyond profit. If an organization values human flourishing as strongly as turning the profit, it will not carelessly use, abuse, and discard people.

The relentless pace of life has robbed us of patience and the ability to focus on long-term growth. We feel that we just don't have time to work with the wounded. We do what a hospital would never do—put the wounded on the street with a pat on the back and a "good luck."

Then there is the problem of communication today. We sometimes lack restraint in what we broadcast with our amazing tools of electronic communication. For some strange reason people's inhibitions are lowered when they type the words of a spicy email or blog post. (And many have had a rude awakening when their email ended up being passed around, or even inadvertently sent directly to the person being criticized.) In our most primitive instincts, it feels good when we are angry or upset to send a sharp-edged email, tweet, or blog post. We say things we would never say if we were face-to-face with the person we are talking about or talking to.

No wonder so many voices are calling for a return to civility today. The work is too big and the stakes are too high for us not to preserve every possible resource—especially the human resources that are needed to bring redemption and restoration to our societies.

Most of us have been wounded, and most of us have wounded someone else. We need the powerful influence of God to reset our thoughts, words, and actions. If we were honest with God, what would we say about all this?

> Lord God, I think we all mean well, but we have made such a mess of things. When life is quiet I look around and I wonder why we make things more complicated than they need to be, why we are so careless, why we don't see the well-being of people around us as the one thing that really matters to you.
>
> We have not been working together. We have not respected each other. We are guilty of comparing, of posturing, and of dismissing each other. I am tired of wasting my energy in these ways. I am ashamed of how I've hurt others; and I'm bleeding from how I've been hurt.

Help me to have the courage to forgive, and to ask for forgiveness from those I have wronged. Help me to forbear the small things that irritate me. Give me a broader and higher vision of what you want to accomplish through your people.

Take away my jealousy and replace it with respect.

Take away my bitterness and grant me your peace.

Take my wounds and heal them.

Take my carelessness and replace it with gentleness.

Lord, your Word says that our struggle is not against people, but against the powers of this dark world and against spiritual forces that want to destroy. Help me to take that seriously. Help me to believe it. And help me—and all the people I have the privilege to serve with—to see evil as the real enemy of humanity.

Lord, flow in your truth and your grace, and flow it out of me.

Amen.

Chapter 18

DEAL WITH CRITICISM

You may find hundreds of faultfinders among professed Christians; but all their criticism will not lead one solitary soul to Christ.

—*Dwight L. Moody*

It felt like a knife penetrating his gut. Lodging there. Tearing more with every move—over days, months, even years. Invisible to people watching. Invisible even to the person who did the stabbing, because he did not think he was doing anything other than being helpful and truthful by offering an honest opinion—to anyone who would listen.

To another leader criticism felt like tiny little darts. There was no one major critic. No malicious backstabbing. But this person sensed that from the day she took the role, she had put on a shirt bearing the image of a target. Almost everyone around had a strong personal opinion about what they agreed with and disagreed with, and (more painfully) what they did or didn't like about her. The commentary about her was continual, and it drifted back to her.

He was a young energetic influencer who easily got his way via charisma and charm. People rarely stood up to him because they did not want to stand in the way of a winner. The momentum of his influence became a self-justifying force, and so he was oblivious to criticism, including constructive criticism. To him the equation was always simple: you're either with me or against me. Decide if you're in the boat or out of the boat. It's my way or the highway. Criticism was not a problem, but *lack* of it *was* a problem, because all the valid discernment, assessment, and critique was blocked. Even worse, the leader was modeling for others that this is the way of effective leadership—full steam ahead and pity the people who get in the way.

It should not surprise us that handling criticism can be extremely difficult. At the moment the leader is criticized he has to discern what others are discerning about him. It is scalpel meeting scalpel. The gift of discernment is sometimes applied as what we call "constructive criticism." But when people are destructively critical, the scalpel becomes the dagger.

The word *criticism* comes from the Greek *krino*, which means "to cut." We are all under the criticism of God. "The word of God is alive and active. Sharper than any double-edged sword, it penetrates even to dividing soul and spirit, joints and marrow; it judges the thoughts and attitudes of the heart" (Heb. 4:12). This is good criticism, an ongoing surgical process that cuts out the bad and gives the good room to grow.

The problem is that human beings are often poor at spiritual surgery. The problem comes in when people let loose with criticism that is nowhere near accurate. And the problem will come up time and again when people have a whole attitude that can only be described as a "critical spirit."

Understanding the Dynamics of Criticism

Instead of understanding the dynamics of criticism, we tend to react to it. However, we need to have tough skins, and one of the best ways to accomplish that is by having a mature, thoughtful, and biblical understanding of why people criticize.

Sometimes people criticize leaders in their attempts to discern whom they can trust. Everyone takes a risk when they trust someone exercising influence in their lives. What if the leader is wrong? Or misguided? Or foolish? Or has the wrong motives? Or is trying to take advantage? Everyone worries about such things because everyone has had bad experiences with leaders. So it should come as no surprise that people will poke and prod and evaluate. That should not be threatening to a leader, who should be able to say, "I understand why you're sizing me up. I know I need to earn your trust. So go ahead and be discerning. Just don't assume the worst while you're doing so. I will tell you this ahead of time: I will make mistakes. But what all of us need is to work together to fix mistakes."

Other times people criticize because they want to feel superior. Criticism can be a power play. Pure and simple. Standing over people with a magnifying glass does not make them bigger; it emphasizes their smallness (in relation to the person holding the magnifying glass). So, people criticize. They examine and probe. They feel empowered by doing so, or protected from being overpowered. Sometimes leaders have set this pattern. Their way of leading is not service but scrutiny. The story can be told many times over of troubled relationships based on cycles of mutual criticism, which is nothing more than a series of power plays.

People criticize when they are searching for truth. After the memo or the speech or the sermon, they seek to cut away the rhetoric and the posturing. They try to unspin the spin. They probe for reality. They want to know the truth. Healthy criticism is a way of getting at reality. This is why we support professional critics: movie critics, food critics, meat inspectors, quality control managers, prophets.

Sometimes people criticize because they have nothing better to do. Boredom is one of the most shameful reasons for criticism. Idleness breeds gossip, and gossip, like a parasite, seeks a host to latch onto. People who have let their lives be about nothing will always have to make their lives be about someone else.

People criticize when they believe leaders are not meeting their needs and expectations. Given the fickle state of human nature, we frequently look at the other and wonder: "What have you done for me lately?" This is especially true of people's expectations of their leaders. Some altruistic people applaud their leaders when they do the right thing, even if it involves cost and sacrifice for everyone. But wise leaders always keep in mind that people's reactions at a base level usually come out of self-interest.

There are other examples, but the main point is this: we should never be shocked or scandalized when we encounter criticism. It comes with the territory. People who can't handle any criticism shouldn't be in positions of influence. A zigzag pattern of criticism, reaction, and reaction to the reaction is a problem for everybody. Overcompensating in the face of criticism distorts the leader's functioning. We should not shrivel up or cower when criticized. A sober self-appraisal is necessary, but this is built over time, the result of listening to the voices of many trusted people who "speak the truth in love." And more important than all that, in spiritual leadership we must believe with everything in us that only God's perspective of us matters. That may produce fear, but "the fear of the LORD is the beginning of knowledge" (Prov. 1:7)—fear in the sense of deep respect. But it also frees us. The knives and the darts don't matter. They may pierce for a moment, but they will fall to the ground. We welcome God's scalpel—the divine discernment and critique—because it always cuts away what is sick and allows us to heal and be stronger than before.

The Key to Dealing with Criticism

It's been months since you were home. Your travel over rugged landscapes and treacherous seas has brought you to a string of strategic destinations. You've tirelessly laid out your message, winning one convert at a time. You're part of a true movement, riding the crest of a wave. You're the most visible person atop it all. But some people in the movement have been relentlessly critical. They have contradicted your message, sought to undermine your reputation with the people you have helped, and even questioned your motives. "He's a loose cannon. He has no proper authority. He's just in it for the money." The criticism comes from fellow workers in the same cause. It isn't careless criticism; it is internecine warfare.

This was the real-life experience of the apostle Paul. While he pushed back the boundaries in his great missionary journeys, his critics tried to undo his work and to undermine his reputation back in Jerusalem. What kept Paul going was a core mindset that set him radically oriented to the will of God, while staying humble in his estimation of himself. He believed that his mission must not be shaped by his critics, but that he must not be arrogantly self-assured. It's a fine line to walk.

One New Testament passage that every Christian leader should know by heart is 1 Corinthians 4:1 – 5. This is the soul-centered resolution Paul came to regarding his efforts, motives, and conscience. It describes a mindset that can keep us tough in the face of wrongful criticism, but soft to the ongoing evaluation of God.

> This, then, is how you ought to regard us: as servants of Christ and as those entrusted with the mysteries God has revealed. Now it is required that those who have been given a trust must prove faithful. I care very little if I am judged by you or by any human court; indeed, I do not even judge myself. My conscience is clear, but that does not make me innocent. It is the Lord who judges me. Therefore judge nothing before the appointed time; wait until the Lord comes. He will bring to light what is hidden in darkness and will expose the motives of the heart. At that time each will receive their praise from God.
>
> —*1 Corinthians 4:1 – 5*

Paul came to these conclusions through much effort and struggle, and they can be grounding principles for anyone today who is called by God to be an influence.

Servanthood, trust, and faithfulness are our calling (we ought to be regarded as "servants of Christ"). We must not care too much when we are judged by others ("I care very little if I am judged by you or by any human court"). We should not be self-obsessed ("I do not even judge myself"), and we should not think our own self-evaluation is infallible ("My conscience is clear, but that does not make me innocent"). The Lord's judgment is all that matters ("judge nothing before the appointed time; wait until the Lord comes"), when everything will come to light, including that most hidden thing: motives ("He will bring to light what is hidden in darkness and will expose the motives of the heart"). In the future we will learn what we did wrong, but also be praised for faithful service, even if others do not see it now ("At that time each will receive their praise from God").

A statement like 1 Corinthians 4:1 – 5 is a pure gift of the grace of God freeing us from scrutiny while binding us to divine guidance. It is a whole mindset. It is protection, and it is motivation.

Practical Steps in Dealing with Criticism

What can you do when you realize you are getting beat up by unfair criticism?

First, evaluate your personal reactions when you're criticized. Bleeding for a week before acknowledging it only makes things worse. Call it what it is. Talk to God about it. Talk to a trusted confidant. If your reaction is anger, recognize that and deal with it constructively. Don't take your anger out on others.

Don't take a defensive posture — especially at the moment of criticism. A coolheaded response is disarming to hot-under-the-collar critics. And a calm response allows you to accept criticism that is fair and accurate.

Don't get caught up in an extended argument. If you feel as though you need to change the mind of every critic, you will waste energy and risk turning resentful. You can say what needs to be said and move on. The other person is responsible for his or her opinions.

Offer a strong, truthful, and even confrontational response if you are quite certain the critic is being destructive. Sometimes leaders need to protect other people (not just themselves) from the rabid critic. But the response should not be an eye for an eye. We have moved past that era.

Take your time in responding to criticism. It may feel good to react verbally — even to get a shot in. But your credibility as a leader and your effectiveness in a conflict hinge on your making a careful, thoughtful, and precise response. Precision is key. In dicey situations a written response is sometimes helpful because you are "going on the record" in an objective way. Write your response, keep it succinct, but hold it for twenty-four hours before sending it. Most of the time you'll end up wanting to revise what you've written or decide not to send anything at all. Resist the temptation to send copies to other people, which is an unfortunate email technique some people use to score points. Damage is multiplied when leaders respond to criticism abruptly and carelessly, and then that gets passed around to others. Then the reaction to the criticism becomes the main issue, and the whole thing looks like a dog chasing its own tail.

Understand the source of the criticism. Many harsh critics are living out their own personal pain. When a leader gets a dart in the chest and has the character to pull it out and calmly ask the critic, "Why did you do that? What is really going on here?" there is an opportunity for the grace and truth of God to curtail a battle before it ever begins. That's a best-case scenario, but it's worth a try.

Use trusted friends and the voice of Scripture to evaluate criticism about important issues. You may conclude that a criticism is unfair, or conversely that it reveals a true problem. Very often you conclude that there is at least a kernel of truth in the criticism. Integrity requires us to accept the truth even when it comes to us in ugly clothing.

Here is one last observation about dealing with criticism. If we do any work that is significant—especially spiritual work—it will create reactions. That will help us reframe the experience of criticism. We can take criticism as a sign that God has allowed us to be a part of something important, something that moves people, something that stirs things up and sometimes produces a knee-jerk oppositional reaction.

Just in case you are at a place in life where you need to know you are not alone in taking the brunt of criticism, consider this: Jonathan Edwards is widely regarded as America's most important theologian and the voice of the Great Awakening, the greatest spiritual revival the country has ever seen. However, Edwards experienced an abrupt ending of his pastoral ministry in Northampton, Massachusetts, when disgruntled congregational members voted him out by a ratio of ten to one. Winston Churchill, who led Great Britain during the dark days of Hitler, was turned out of office within a year of the end of World War II. Steve Jobs, an inventor whose innovations in several major industries give him a rank near that of Thomas Edison, was fired by the board of Apple Computer just as he was getting started with his digital revolution. Now, each of these circumstances was complicated, and strong personalities dominated, but they remind us that there will always be battles in leadership. Critics will raise their voices, those criticized will dig their trenches, and the big picture is often obscured.

All the more reason for us to trade in the dull-edged sword of criticism for the razor-sharp scalpel of discernment—and to ask God to do the work.

Chapter 19

BUILD PAST FAILURE

Success consists of going from failure to failure without loss of enthusiasm.
— *Winston Churchill*

The single sentence that came crackling through the radio signal from almost a quarter-million miles from Earth sounded simple, even routine. "Houston, we've had a problem." The three crew members of the *Apollo 13* spacecraft circling the moon knew that something had gone terribly wrong with their spacecraft after hearing the sound of an explosion and watching their electricity-generating fuel cells go dead. "A problem" for sure. The planned moon landing was aborted and emergency measures were put in place for the crew to coax their crippled craft back toward Earth. Three days later the capsule splashed down in the Pacific. NASA called the mission "a successful failure." Commander James Lovell told the tale in a book with a mournful-sounding title: *Lost Moon.*

Another sentence voiced from the moon ten months earlier is equally memorable: "Houston, Tranquility Base here—the *Eagle* has landed." Neil Armstrong, commander of *Apollo 11*, had manually controlled the landing vehicle over boulder-strewn plains to a safe landing on the lunar surface. More people on Earth were focused on that moment than any other event in history. For the first time ever, a thrill and celebration broke out across all humanity. Two men landing a thin-skinned spidery metal box on another planetary body was a success almost beyond imagining.

One a "success" and the other a "successful failure."

Yet decades after the Apollo project, it was a film telling of the story of the "successful failure," *Apollo 13*, that won widespread acclaim. Ron Howard's movie gives the inside story of how three men trapped in a fragile, cramped spacecraft hundreds of thousands of miles from Earth were able to overcome a lack of oxygen, water, and electricity to limp back to Earth. They improvised perilous rocket burns to put them on the right trajectory. They rebuilt mechanical systems in the craft. And dozens of young engineers, computer programmers, aeronautics experts, and others worked together to move past the failure of the spacecraft. Not many people today even remember that, in total, there were six successful moon landings in the Apollo program, that twelve different men walked on the moon. They probably do remember, however, something about the "successful failure."

Success is not about avoiding or denying failure. It is about building past failure. If "success" means little if any failure, then the only way to achieve it is to never try anything new. Certainly nothing bold or risky.

Failure Is Inevitable

We might not want to deal with failure—just focus on one accomplishment after the other, don't let disappointments distract, and move forward on the path of least resistance. But this would not be good leadership. There are numerous reasons failure is not entirely a bad thing.

Admitting failure is to live in reality. Influencers who live with the fantasy that they have never made mistakes just look ridiculous. They have a hard time gaining credibility in the eyes of others because everyone watching wants to learn how to move past their own failures.

Dealing with failure is not the occasional distraction from our mission; it is the mission. The metanarrative of Scripture goes from creation to fall to redemption to glory. Living as we do in the age of redemption means that life is a continual battle to suppress sin, defeat ignorance, and restore relationships. That is, to build past failure.

Moving past failure is the norm in all biblical examples of leadership. A young Moses killed a man as a vigilante act. David committed adultery and had a disastrous family life. Solomon started out wise, but became addicted to his own success. Elijah the prophet stood up to the prophets of Baal, but ran away from a wrathful woman. Peter denied Jesus three times. On his great missionary journeys, Paul experienced one success after another, but also had long periods when no one was responding, and had to deal with broken relationships with his fellow Christian leaders at every turn.

Besides these and hundreds of other examples in Scripture of dealing with failure, there is an underlying biblical theology of dealing with failure, which shapes the purpose of spiritual influence. We are broken creatures living in a broken world. The evidence of that is as diverse as disease, war, child abuse, divorce, addiction, economic injustice, and earthquakes. In the face of such forces human leadership is incomplete. But the creator of the universe, out of compassion, is on a campaign of restoration. God is the influence; God is the leader. He uses people as his instruments in this great campaign. In taking up the task of spiritual leadership, we join the battles against ignorance, sin, and inequity. And along the way we will have to deal with our own failures.

Different Kinds of Failure

To deal with our failures we need to gain an honest assessment of what they really mean. Different kinds of failures require different kinds of responses.

Was this an unintentional or intentional failure? We know that unknowing mistakes are not as wrongful as fully intentional transgressions. So we will always be tempted to describe our failures simply as mistakes. But we would all do well never to use that all-too-common platitude: "I know I'm not a perfect person." Saying that we are less than divine hardly qualifies as an honest assessment of failure. Most of the people around us have already figured out that we are not Jesus.

Just because a failure is unintentional does not mean its effects are minimal. A budgeting mistake borne of inexperience can bankrupt a company. A bit of gossip "innocently" passed on can be a spark at the beginning of a forest fire. Naive theology can undermine the strength of a church body.

The reason this point even needs to be made — that unintentional mistakes can lead to major problems — is that we struggle with figuring out the balance between grace and responsibility. There are leaders who have perfectionistic streaks, but there are also leaders who, under the umbrella of grace, shrug their shoulders when they make mistakes and doom themselves to making more unnecessary mistakes in the future. God is patient and forgiving (a truth made abundantly clear in the lives of leaders in the Bible), but if we presume on that, we put our leadership in peril.

Is this a onetime or a long-term failure? Patterns matter. If the people closest to us point out an error or shortcoming in us, and it is an issue that has come up many times in the past, we need to connect the dots. This is important: all of us will at some point take on a task or responsibility that is beyond our capabilities or gifts. We will come up short. We can keep on trying, but the result will not change if we have risen to the level of our incompetence. The solution is for us to bring the talents of other people to bear on the issue, or to step out of the role.

Is the failure moral or practical? Morality is a set of boundary lines that swing dramatically depending on who you talk to. Marital infidelity is not likely to cost a political leader in France his job. Corruption and graft are the norm in most African countries. In the US many sins of avarice are covered in the name of capitalism. In the world of leadership, in other words, few actions are universally condemned as moral failures.

Spiritual influence is different. One of the central goals of spiritual influence is to help people engage with God their creator so that the process of being remade into the image of God can happen. So morality is central. And it is not just a list of do's and don'ts.

One of the most heart-wrenching issues that comes up all too often is sexual immorality. While most people do not question the disqualification of a leader who has been discovered to have been blatantly promiscuous, it is another story when a leader has had a onetime inappropriate sexual involvement. When sexual moral failures are uncovered, there are often two different reactions: rejection borne out of a sense of personal betrayal, or forgiveness and forbearance when there is a strong personal connection.

When we are dealing with a moral crisis, we need to help people distinguish two distinct issues: personal forgiveness and leadership qualification. Biblical theology is abundantly clear that there are no unforgivable sins. Sexual immorality may be an especially devastating transgression—shattering marriage covenants, undermining the institution of the family, robbing faithfulness in relationships—but it does not cut people off from the grace of God. And so people may be heartbroken to learn of the moral failure of a friend, but glad when that person humbly makes their way back to God with authentic contrition.

God's forgiveness does not necessarily mean restoration to leadership responsibility. In some cases the person ought to be permanently disqualified (for instance, a teacher found to be physically or sexually abusive to children should never teach again—ever). In other cases the person may be restored to leadership after an appropriate time of moral restoration (a hospital administrator comes back to work after a disciplinary forced leave). And in still other situations someone may come back into leadership, but in a different form or context (a pastor who got into a sexual relationship with a volunteer leaves church ministry, but becomes a fund-raiser for a national ministry after several years of moral reparation).

It is hard to deal with such situations without turning into Pharisees. There are no exact laws in Scripture in dealing with moral failure because legalism does not produce holiness. Each situation needs to be approached seriously, respectfully, and cautiously, seeking the grace and truth of Christ each step of the way.

Wrestling with the Sense of Failure

When we are honest we will admit to God and to the appropriate people in our lives when we have failed at any level. There is just no reason to hold back—though almost every one of us does. (This is not to say that every failure is everybody's business.) Pretending we are something that we are not simply sets us up for the most devastating failure of all—some calamitous fall because of pride.

But on the other hand there is this problem: when we live with a constant sense of inadequacy, guilt, and failure, we are hobbled. We should have humility, but we cannot lead out of a sense of humiliation. "Failure" is not supposed to be an identity.

And as if this isn't complicated enough, some leaders who feel profoundly insecure compensate with a forced self-confidence. It is the worst of both worlds: inadequacy clothed in bravado. It may be more common than any of us imagine.

Here are some practical steps in dealing with a pervasive sense of failure:

When we know that we are recovering from some significant failure on our part, we should accept the embarrassment and self-disappointment, but process what happened with trusted friends, coworkers, mentors, or other counselors. It might be helpful for us to think of this like a grief process. Ecclesiastes 7:2–4 talks about going into "the house of mourning" for a season. It is not where we are meant to live permanently, but it is the appropriate state of mind while we work through the sense of loss that always accompanies failure.

When we are coming through failure, we should turn this period into a time of learning. The wisest and best leaders have learned from their mistakes instead of denying them. It is painful when we review a time of failure, especially as it uncovers our own shortcomings. But when we do so, with other people who are fair-minded, trustworthy, and perceptive, we will be in a better state to move on.

Learn caution through failure, but do not become overly cautious. There is a fine balance here. Some failures teach us where we were careless, overly ambitious, or overconfident, and so the failure teaches us to rein ourselves in. But if we play it too safe as we move ahead, then the failure has effectively shut us down.

When we have a sense of failure but other people we trust assure us that it is just our self-perception, not based in reality, then we have to figure out where that insecurity is coming from. It may come from a string of disappointments that have produced a pervasive sense of nervousness. It may come from experiences in an entirely different area of life—like a leader struggling in a marriage—and that results in a sense of failure everywhere. Sometimes insecurity is a matter of temperament. It has been there all along, lurking under the surface.

Dealing with Failure Today

Today's culture does not help us deal with failure in healthy ways. The pace and impatience and superficiality of our culture make dealing with failure an inconvenience. It is challenging enough to be brave about honestly looking at failure, but the tyranny of "the next thing" causes us to short-circuit the process (or gives us a convenient excuse not to deal with failure). Here is some of what we are up against:

The quick-fix mentality. The pace of life today has made us more impatient, and so we look for quick fixes when we ought to sit down in the school of failure, work through the issues, and gradually get back on our feet.

The bottom-line mentality. When all endeavors are measured by numeric results, we will miss some of the most important successes, which are intangible. We will evaluate numerically small results as failures. And we might be blind to far more profound failures of character which ought to be getting our attention. Jesus' earthly ministry, judged by the spreadsheet, was a failure.

The superficial mentality. Today we evaluate our efforts by the quick glance at the externals: the image, the brand, the buy-in. We substitute public relations for personal credibility. We focus on physical health before spiritual health. We exchange winning for faithfulness.

This is sobering. We know these are our issues today. Leaders talk about them in conferences. But it's another thing to do something about our unhealthy patterns. Sadly, it sometimes takes a heart attack, a moral failure, or a bankruptcy to get our attention and to get us to recalibrate our leadership efforts.

On a more positive note, if we renew our commitment to spiritual influence, taking a fresh view of the dramatic biblical paradigm of submission and service, reaffirming that God is the only leader of enduring influence and we are his instruments, it is possible for us to deal with devastating failures. A chapter here and there of our lives may not turn out according to our expectations, but God is writing the whole story.

Chapter 20

SANCTIFY AMBITION

Ambition is a dream with a V-8 engine.

—*Elvis Presley*

People who are powerful influences on others are driven by a strong desire. But here is where motive is everything. A selfless, exuberant ambition propels us forward. But ambition that is a drive to grab and possess automatically spoils spiritual leadership, even though the rottenness may be invisible to the crowds.

For most people the word *ambition* elicits some kind of gut-level reaction. For some, the word implies a positive sense of energy, drive, and purposefulness. Others automatically react negatively. They see ambition as the outworking of pride and arrogance. It is selfish and showy. It is a bull that will take you for a ride and throw you to the ground.

In Christian circles we have mixed feelings about ambition. For some, it is godly vision and passion; for others, it is shameless competition or greed. Our reaction to it is usually formed by our past experiences with people of sanctified ambition or selfish ambition. And the truth is, most of us have experienced both.

The most powerful dynamics of influence issue from the core of human nature, and so it comes as no surprise that ambition is an expression of created human nature—being made in the image of God. We are ambitious because God is ambitious. We work because God works. We have a drive toward excellence because God does. We are not satisfied with the status quo because God is not.

Then again, the twist in the human soul that is sin causes our ambition all too often to devolve into something primitive and dark. The Tower of Babel is the story of godless ambition. It took a lot of ambition to try to build a tower that reached to heaven, a blind ambition founded on a low view of God and an exaggerated view of human ability.[1]

In essence, ambition is simply a strong desire to achieve something. It is determination, drive, and hard work. What matters is how it is applied, the motive behind it, and the goals toward which it is aimed.

A young businessman goes to a trusted spiritual advisor with a dilemma. He explains that he has an insatiable drive to grow his company and make as much money as possible. He says he knows that he is driven by a certain salary goal, but he says that his real satisfaction comes from knowing that the success of his company means that he can give gainful employment to more and more men and women. He is honestly confused. Is his ambition a good thing or a bad thing?

A middle-aged pastor who is used to having the largest church in town is stunned by the sudden growth of two newer congregations. He starts using new techniques to get people through the door, and it is working. He believes that it honors God to reach out to more people, but in his heart of hearts he knows he is driven by competitiveness and insecurity. He is looking over his shoulder at other churches and their leaders. He feels guilty about that, but he also wonders whether competition is necessarily a bad thing.

A woman takes a job leading a small organization. Fairly quickly she spots significant opportunities for expansion and growth. But the culture of the organization is very conservative and resistant to

---

1. The New Testament word frequently translated "ambition" means "strong desire" (*epithumeo*). Sometimes it is used for a drive to fulfill God's purpose, but the same word is used to mean "lust" or "covetousness."

change. When she introduces new horizons, she is accused of being overly ambitious and of abandoning the core value of faithful work in the organization. She is confused and hurt. She knows what her motives are — so why do other people have to accuse her of over-reaching? And why are the accusations so personal?

Eager or Reluctant?

"Here is a trustworthy saying: Whoever aspires to be an overseer desires a noble task" (1 Tim. 3:1). That's the advice the apostle Paul gave his young associate Timothy, whom he had charged with finding and recruiting leaders in the important city of Ephesus, where Paul had worked for years. As part of the process, Paul stipulates the basic requirements for service (1 Tim. 3:2 – 12), but there is also this background issue: What do you do with the aspirations of potential leaders? How do you distinguish the called from those who merely want positions of influence?

It would be easy to assume that the starting place for leadership is the longing to do it. But then again, some of the best leaders the world has ever seen have been reluctant to take up the charge. If being ambitious to lead were a prerequisite for leadership, then one of the greatest leaders in the history of the world would have lived and died in obscurity: Moses. He was honest with God: "Please send someone else" (Exod. 4:13). Part of Moses' reluctance was the public face of leadership. He knew that it meant using words in public, and he felt completely incapable of that. "I have never been eloquent.... I am slow of speech" (Exod. 4:10).

Centuries later a man named Jeremiah was called by God to carry out a prophetic role. His response? "I do not know how to speak; I am too young" (Jer. 1:6).

The story can be told many times over. Men and women of great capabilities being called to positions of power and influence, but being intimidated by a daunting task. When Harry Truman became president of the United States after the death of Franklin Delano Roosevelt, he said privately that he felt like the sky, sun, moon, and all of the stars had fallen on his shoulders. When Gerald Ford became president after the resignation of Richard Nixon, nobody accused him of positioning for power. Colin Powell—chairman of the joint chiefs of staff, national security advisor, and secretary of state—called himself "the reluctant general" because he viewed war as a failure of democracy. In each case once responsibility was cast on them, these people took the challenge, even though it was not personal ambition that brought them there.

Highly capable, wise people may be reluctant to take a position of influence because they are wise enough to know that a great personal cost is often involved, and they are not interested in getting status or power at any cost. That is one reason to be careful about people who have an enormous drive to get into positions of influence. Is it the good of others that they have in mind—which is gained only by labor and sacrifice—or is it prestige and position?

So, going back to "Whoever aspires to be an overseer desires a noble task" (1 Tim. 3:1), we should notice several things. *Aspiring* has the meaning of desiring, longing for, stretching out for. The other two times this particular word is used in the New Testament refer to desiring heaven (Heb. 11:16) and greed (1 Tim. 6:10, "love of money"), so aspirations can be noble or ignoble. "Noble task" means a good work, an investment of time and energy toward a worthy goal.

So the ambition to lead is a good thing when it is desire attached to the right end. Even reluctant leaders in the end make the choice to respond to the call. And if they stay dependent on God, their ambition will drive them to work that honors God.

To those on the outside it may be very difficult to know what those motives are. Sometimes leaders with good motives are arbitrarily perceived as being self-serving, and sometimes leaders with selfish motives are really good at masking their hearts. Only God knows the heart, although we should listen to people with discernment who sound alarm bells about ambitious influencers who may be leading people down the wrong path.

Ambition Sanctified

Simon Peter is the prototype of well-intentioned ambition. At every turn Peter jumped at any opportunity to lunge ahead in the cause. First to answer a question, first to jump out of the boat, first to draw a sword.

Jesus never chastised Peter for his ambition. He tempered it and directed it. When Peter swore that he would follow Jesus anywhere, Jesus warned him of difficult days ahead. Jesus washed Peter's feet—though Peter was reluctant at first, then overeager. Leaving the upper room to go into the night, Peter assured Jesus that he had weapons on hand. Jesus' reply: "That's enough," meaning, "Calm down, Peter. Put your feet on the ground; open your eyes."

But it was in a conversation after the resurrection that Jesus really sanctified Peter's ambition. Jesus asks Peter three times, "Do you love me?" Eager replies follow, three times over. Yes! Yes! Of course, yes! Jesus then puts Peter on the trajectory toward spiritual influence, three times over: "Then feed my lambs.... Take care of my sheep.... Feed my sheep" (see John 21:15–17). In other words, "Peter, your ambition will be fine, as long as it is aligned to my heart and directed toward those I have a heart for."

This biblical text encapsulates the whole paradigm of spiritual leadership. Jesus is the real leader, the true influence. He is intent on caring for people—his sheep and lambs. He invites his disciple to be the instrument of that sweeping, loving, saving movement. Jesus is ambitious for the well-being of people whom he has rescued; and he invites us to be driven by that same ambition.

There is no ambiguity about the mission of the people of God and their leaders. It is so much easier to let the ambition of God flow into us and then to flow out of us than it is to try to generate our own energy. And it is the right thing to do.

The first epistle of Peter offers the same perspective: "Be shepherds of God's flock that is under your care, watching over them—not because you must, but *because you are willing*, as God wants you to be; not pursuing dishonest gain, but *eager to serve*" (1 Peter 5:2, emphasis added). Compulsion is tamed by calling. Rapacity is nullified by service. Ambition can be sanctified as spiritual influence settles out as shepherding care.

Walking Lightly in the Halls of Power

One man has proclaimed the good news of Jesus to more people in the world than any other person in history. Over a period of six decades, he was sought by the men who have been president of the United States. He walked through open doors of foreign heads of state, leaders of industry, and religious leaders of every sort. Hundreds of millions of households knew him through the television screen. And all this happened because Billy Graham is a most ambitious man. But he was voted the most respected man in America year after year because it was apparent to all that he was also the humblest of leaders. Darting around the world came at great personal sacrifice. He never lived in luxury. He was willing to step into the limelight, not because it served his ego, but because it served his message. No one can know the deepest motives of other people, but our motives have a way of leaking out. Graham simply came off as sincere in every respect—a quality that is hard to fake. He was captivated by the message of the saving work of Christ. Not just captivated, but possessed, compelled, and convicted. Fame was an awkward by-product.

Billy Graham had to have ambition—a drive, a desire, a hunger—otherwise he would not have stayed for weeks at a time preaching in revival meetings in large tents. He would not have experimented with the new communication platform of television in the 1950s, and committed to national broadcasts. He would not have been able to raise hundreds of millions of dollars. He would not have started publications like *Decision* magazine and *Christianity Today*. He would not have founded schools.

Is it possible to have enormous ambition, and for it not to corrupt a personality? Billy Graham's story suggests so.

What to Do about Ambition

So how do people who want to be spiritual influences stoke the fire of ambition, but make sure it stays under control?

First, we must be captivated by the truth of God in Christ, and carried along by the movement of the Spirit of God in the world. We must have a sense of wonder and awe about it. We must see ourselves as tiny ships on a great sea with stiff winds. We must keep ourselves in perspective. Then it is possible to have an enormous amount of ambition, because it is directed into the mission of God and is energized by the power of God.

Second, our ambition can increase if we accumulate "wins," that is, when we are energized by the fruits of good work. Satisfaction from a job well done has an invigorating effect. We should take time to celebrate accomplishments, always giving credit to everyone who had a hand in a successful endeavor. If we just rush off to the next task, we've missed an opportunity to recharge our ambitions.

Third, we should join with others in the work of spiritual influence. The solo leader, the one detached or walled off from other leaders, is always at greatest risk of being blind about the motives behind his or her ambitions. The longer someone leads, the greater the danger that he or she will live in a bubble. Human nature causes us to gather people who like us and who are like us, people who reinforce our own agendas. Alternative perspectives are pushed to the background. Proper ambition turns into blind ambition. And then blind ambition becomes what the writers of the epistles call "selfish ambition."

Fourth, ambition must be joined to wisdom—that foundation of values that keeps us focused on what is good and keeps us connected with the mind of God. The book of James says: "Who is wise and understanding among you? Let them show it by their good life, by deeds done in the humility that comes from wisdom. But if you harbor bitter envy and selfish ambition in your hearts, do not boast about it or deny the truth. Such 'wisdom' does not come down from heaven but is earthly, unspiritual, demonic. For where you have envy and selfish ambition, there you find disorder and every evil practice" (James 3:13–16).

Fifth, we must ask God to increase our ambition. If we have our wits about us and our values grounded in the ethics of the kingdom of God, we have every reason to be more ambitious. Ambition generated by God makes a leader like an ox pulling a plow, rather than a bull out of control.

Opportunities for Godly Ambition

Today's world offers exciting new possibilities for godly ambition to be attached to purposes consistent with the kingdom of God. Globalization has made it possible for a work with spiritual integrity to explore cross-cultural dimensions almost immediately. The ambition and ability of many people to travel the world, in the past confined to an elite class, makes it possible for cross-cultural experiences and relationships to mature many different spiritual initiatives. The democratization of communication through the internet has made it possible for ambitious people to form new networks and virtual relationships (that hopefully will lead to real relationships) with little expense and little time lag. Amazing new creative enterprises developed by ambitious entrepreneurs can now be attempted in a small way, without the delay of building a complicated infrastructure — for instance the many humanitarian projects that have been created by connecting people with resources to people with needs.

Sanctified ambition makes it possible for multitudes of people whose names will never be highly publicized, who will never write a book or found an organization, to be part of initiatives that will transform lives. First Thessalonians 4:11 – 12 describes the "every person" kind of ambition that may just be the great story of spiritual initiative today: "Make it your ambition to lead a quiet life: You should mind your own business and work with your hands, just as we told you, so that your daily life may win the respect of outsiders."

Some Final Words

When five-year-old Albert Einstein encountered a compass with that magical pointer that moved like an invisible hand was directing it, he felt a sense of wonder that stuck with him his whole life. This conviction that "something deeply hidden had to be behind things" was central to the passion and curiosity that drove him to understand the physical universe and to produce work that won him *Time*'s label as the most influential person of the twentieth century.

Of course the compass has a symbolic significance that goes beyond hidden power. A compass points in a direction. It gives bearings. It tells a person where they are in the world. Compasses guide ships and save hikers. They give comfort.

Now apply the analogy to spiritual leadership. If it is true that there is a creator God who did far more than fashion the magnetic fields of planets, whose hidden power is life and light and goodness, health and wholeness, harmony and connectedness — then is there anything more influential people could need today? And is there anything more constructive that can shape the life of organizations, companies, and even nations?

We do need people who will respond to the call of spiritual influence. Not just a few we elect into office or hire as CEOs or put on national television. We need armies of influencers who understand that their highest calling is to seek enduring effects in people's lives, not just to get people to do things. We need many because we need proximity. Ask people to name the person who has been the greatest spiritual influence in their lives and they will almost always name someone whom they knew face-to-face. Someone who talked directly to them. A pattern of millions of such connections—person to person, face to face—is our best hope for transformation.

Influence and leadership begin with the forces at work deep within us before we ever start to influence others. The kingdom of God may start small like a mustard seed, but it pervades like leaven, changing all areas of life. How God can use people as mixed up as we are is a mystery. That he even wants to is a marvel.

CONCLUSION
WHERE DO WE GO FROM HERE?

In this book we've talked about twenty different themes that fit into (a) getting grounded, (b) taking initiative, (c) going deep, and (d) facing challenges. Each of us will go through phases in which one or the other of these dynamics is most important.

One person will think, "I really need to get more fully connected with God. To learn or relearn what it is to follow Christ. To build the integrity of my personal life. I have been trying to be a good influence, but I've not appreciated the power of God's influence on me first."

Another will say, "I need to get into action, to take initiative on what I already possess. I know what is right. I know what needs to be done. This is not a time to hesitate. The needs are too great. The stakes are too high. I hear the voice of God challenging me to exercise influence by seizing opportunities, by exploring some new horizons, by being bold enough to do justice and love mercy."

Yet another person will have this conviction: "I need to go deeper. My influence and leadership have been superficial. Merely pragmatic. I know I need to apprehend the deep wisdom of God—and his power, authority, and truth. I need to stop flexing my muscles, and instead tie into the immense and mysterious power of the Spirit of God. I don't just want to influence people by moving bodies around. I want to be used by God to have an enduring effect in people's lives."

And a different person will think: "I realize now I am limited by challenges I need to face. I have paid more attention to the expectations of people than the expectations of God. I did not realize that I have been bleeding from wounds, crippled by criticism, or paralyzed by a sense of failure. I need God's patience, forgiveness, support, and guidance. I know I need to persevere and plod."

It cannot be said too strongly: given the state of the world in which we live, we need armies of believers to rise up and be powerful spiritual influences. In every arena of society—in the church, in the marketplace, in education, in community life, in the family—we need people who have received the deep things of God and who pass them on. We need followers of Christ who are thirsty and who long to help everyone else who is thirsty: "Let anyone who is thirsty come to me and drink. Whoever believes in me, as Scripture has said, rivers of living water will flow out from within them" (John 7:37).

We need business leaders who place a value on building people at the same time that they build the bottom line. We need teachers who, out of their faith, bring wisdom and not just knowledge to their students. We need pastors who make every effort to discern spiritual movements within their congregations and discover God's leading for the future. We need medical care workers who respect the whole person. We need social reformers who will take risks to stand for justice in dangerous circumstances and who will commit to decades of work to dent the conscience of society. We need publishers who tell the truth, legal advocates who have impeccable ethics, mass media professionals who develop messages with real meaning. We need parents who understand that they influence their children so deeply every day that they will seek the sanctifying power of the Spirit.

Most important, we need influencers who care. Leaders who are noisy gongs and clanging cymbals (1 Cor. 13:1) are easy to come by. What we need are influencers who understand Jesus' ultimate call to love him by loving those he loves (John 21:15–17). We need followers of Christ who share his vision of human need: "Jesus went through all the towns and villages, teaching in their synagogues, proclaiming the good news of the kingdom and healing every disease and sickness. When he saw the crowds, he had compassion on them, because they were harassed and helpless, like sheep without a shepherd. Then he said to his disciples, 'The harvest is plentiful but the workers are few. Ask the Lord of the harvest, therefore, to send out workers into his harvest field'" (Matt. 9:35–37).

It is one thing to realize that you can influence other people; it is another to be driven by a compassion that will cause you to influence for the right reason. This means influencing because we allow ourselves to be burdened, brokenhearted, and frustrated because there is no other way to close the gap. We accept the reality that things are not the way they are supposed to be—and then we reject the idea that we will leave things that way. We look out at the scenes in our neighborhoods, our churches, our countries, our world—and a deep longing makes our souls ache. And then we get to work.

Look for extended resources for this book at
www.theinfluenceproject.com.

For other writings and
resources from Mel Lawrenz...

SHARING IDEAS,
PURSUING WISDOM.

_____

thebrooknetwork.org

FOR MORE TOOLS TO
Deepen Your Influence

AND TO FORM YOUR OWN
Circle of Influence

THEINFLUENCEPROJECT.COM